"Os Guinness is a prophet. Hear him."

Eric Metaxas, *New York Times*–bestselling author of *Bonhoeffer: Pastor, Martyr, Prophet, Spy*

"Every time I sit down to read the prophetic words of Os Guinness, I feel my spine strengthen and my mind perk up. His clear writing and earned wisdom bring both courage and uncertainty; for while we can't predict where our culture will head, we can rely on the truth that guides and emboldens every generation to meet the moment for which we've been called."

Gabe Lyons, founder of Q, author of *Good Faith*

"I read everything Os Guinness writes because he always challenges my thinking and enlarges my perspective. *Impossible People* may be his most important work. Read it, then buy five copies for friends and discuss it together. The message is that important. This could be the most important book you read this year."

Rick Warren, pastor, Saddleback Church, author of *The Purpose Driven Life*

"This remarkable book helps us to clearly see how Western modernity is trying to replace Christian faith with a progressive secularism. It is a timely wake-up call for the church to stand firm against this fatal challenge. I urge every Christian leader to read it."

Mouneer Anis, primate of the Anglican Province of Jerusalem and the Middle East

"With his unique blend of incisive clarity and prophetic vision, Os Guinness has written a book that will challenge, encourage and awaken us to live wholeheartedly for Christ in this 'grand clarifying moment.' I recommend *Impossible People* as a book for such a time as this."

Amy Orr-Ewing, director, The Oxford Centre for Christian Apologetics

IMPOSSIBLE
PEOPLE

CHRISTIAN COURAGE AND THE STRUGGLE FOR THE SOUL OF CIVILIZATION

OS GUINNESS

IVP Books

An imprint of InterVarsity Press
Downers Grove, Illinois

InterVarsity Press
P.O. Box 1400, Downers Grove, IL 60515-1426
ivpress.com
email@ivpress.com

InterVarsity Press® is the book-publishing division of InterVarsity Christian Fellowship/USA®, a
movement of students and faculty active on campus at hundreds of universities, colleges and schools
of nursing in the United States of America, and a member movement of the International Fellowship
of Evangelical Students. For information about local and regional activities, visit intervarsity.org.

All Scripture quotations, unless otherwise indicated, are taken from the New American Standard
Bible®, copyright 1960, 1962, 1963, 1968, 1971, 1972, 1973, 1975, 1977, 1995 by The Lockman
Foundation. Used by permission.

While any stories in this book are true, some names and identifying information may have been
changed to protect the privacy of individuals.

Published in association with the literary agency of Wolgemuth & Associates.

Cover design: Cindy Kiple
Interior design: Beth McGill
Images: Colosseum: © neirfy/iStockphoto
        Colosseum illustration: © alesnowak/iStockphoto

ISBN 978-0-8308-4465-4 (print)
ISBN 978-0-8308-9338-6 (digital)

Printed in the United States of America ∞

Library of Congress Cataloging-in-Publication Data
Names: Guinness, Os, author.
Title: Impossible people : Christian courage and the struggle for the soul of
    civilization / Os Guinness.
Description: Downers Grove : InterVarsity Press, 2016. | Includes
    ibliographical references and index.
Identifiers: LCCN 2016010689 (print) | LCCN 2016011225 (ebook) | ISBN
    9780830844654 (hardcover : alk. paper) | ISBN 9780830893386 (eBook)
Subjects: LCSH: Christian life. | Christianity and culture—History—21st
    century.
Classification: LCC BV4501.3 .G849 2016 (print) | LCC BV4501.3 (ebook) | DDC
    270.8/3—dc23
LC record available at http://lccn.loc.gov/2016010689

P	20	19	18	17	16	15	14	13	12	11	10	9	8	7	6	5	4	3	2	1
Y	33	32	31	30	29	28	27	26	25	24	23	22	21	20	19	18	17	16

DOM

And to Dick and Mary Ohman,

—true friends, without whom.

Contents

Introduction: Found Faithful / 21

1 New World, Old Challenge / 37

2 The Greatest Challenge Ever / 62

3 The War of Spirits / 90

4 Exploring the Heart of Darkness / 115

5 Life with No Amen / 142

6 Yesterday, Today, Forever / 169

7 Give Us the Tools / 195

Afterword: A Time to Stand / 215

Notes / 225

Name Index / 233

Subject Index / 235

Scripture Index / 237

The Lord said, "Behold, they are one people, and they all have the same language. And this is what they began to do, and now nothing which they purpose to do will be impossible for them. Come, let Us go down and there confuse their language, so that they will not understand one another's speech." So the LORD scattered them abroad from there over the face of the whole earth; and they stopped building the city. Therefore its name was called Babel, because there the LORD confused the language of the whole earth.

GENESIS 11:6-9

If the foundations are destroyed,
What can the righteous do?

PSALM 11:3

I am the LORD, that is My name;
I will not give My glory to another.

ISAIAH 42:8

Because your heart is lifted up
And you have said, "I am a god,
I sit in the seat of gods
In the heart of the seas";
Yet you are a man and not God,
Although you make your heart like the heart of God.

EZEKIEL 28:2

I heard a mighty voice crying from the elements of the world:
"We cannot move and complete our accustomed rounds as
we should do according to the precepts of our Creator. For
humankind, because of its corruptions, spins us about like
the sails of a windmill. And so now we stink from pestilence
and from hunger after justice." As often as the elements of the
world are violated by ill-treatment, God will cleanse them
by the sufferings and hardships of humankind. . . . All of cre-
ation God gives to humankind to use. But if this privilege is
misused, God's justice permits creation to punish humanity.

HILDEGARD OF BINGEN,
MEDITATIONS WITH HILDEGARD OF BINGEN

I have placed you at the very center of the world, so that from
that vantage point you may with greater ease glance around
you on all the world contains. We have made you a creature
neither of heaven nor of earth, neither mortal nor immortal,
in order that you may, as the free and proud shaper of your
own being, fashion yourself in the form you may prefer. It will
be in your power to descend to the lower, brutish forms of life;
you will be able, through your own decision, to rise again to
the superior orders whose life is divine.

PICO DELLA MIRANDOLA,
ORATION ON THE DIGNITY OF MAN

Man must . . . venerate the state as a secular deity.

GEORGE HEGEL,
THE PHILOSOPHY OF RIGHT

To be a nation . . . is the religion of our time. Leave all the little religions and perform the great duty to the single highest, and unite yourself in it to one belief high above the pope or Luther. That is the ultimate religion.

ERNST ARNDT,
GEIST DER ZEIT

*The beginning, middle and
end of religion is MAN.*

LUDWIG FEUERBACH,
THE ESSENCE OF CHRISTIANITY

*Man is free only if he owes his existence to himself. . . .
Philosophy makes no secret of it. Prometheus' admission
"I hate all gods" is its own admission, its own motto against
all gods, heavenly and earthly, who do not acknowledge
the consciousness of man as the supreme divinity.*

KARL MARX,
DOCTORAL THESIS

In some isolated corner of the universe, poured out shimmer-ingly into unaccountable solar systems, there was once a star upon which clever animals invented knowledge. It was the most arrogant and hypocritical minute of "world history": but it was only a minute. After nature drew a few breaths, the star grew stiff with cold, and the clever animals had to die.

FRIEDRICH NIETZSCHE,
"TRUTH AND LIE IN A MORALLY DISENGAGED SENSE"

Should I eat and drink, only in order to hunger and thirst again, and eat and drink, merely until the open grave under my feet swallows me up as a meal for the earth? Should I create more beings like myself, so that they can eat and drink and die, and so they can leave behind beings of their own, so that they do the same as I have already done? What is the point of this continual, self-contained and ever-returning circle, this repetitive game that always starts again in the same way, in which everything is, in order to fade away, and fades away in order to return again as it was—this monster continually devouring itself in order to reproduce itself, and reproduce itself in order to devour itself?

JOHANN GOTTLIEB FICHTE,
THE VOCATION OF MAN

The West has lost Christ, and that is why it is dying; that is the only reason.

FYODOR DOSTOEVSKY,
NOTEBOOKS

Where there is no God, there is no man either.

NICHOLAS BERDYAEV,
A NEW MIDDLE AGES?

Once acclimatized to space-living, it is unlikely that man will stop until he has roamed over and colonized most of the sidereal universe, or that even this will be the end. Man will not ultimately be content to be parasitic on the stars, but will invade them and organize them for his own purposes. . . . The stars cannot be allowed to continue in their old way, but will be turned into efficient heat engines. . . . By intelligent organization, the life of the universe could probably be prolonged to many millions of millions of times what it would be without organization.

J. D. BERNAL,
THE WORLD, THE FLESH AND THE DEVIL

Some day we will realize that the prime duty, the inescapable citizen of the right type is to leave his or her blood behind him in the world; and that we have no business to permit the perpetuation of citizens of the wrong type. The great problem of civilization is to secure a relative increase of the valuable as compared with the less valuable or noxious elements in the population. . . . I wish very much that the wrong people could be prevented entirely from breeding, and when the evil nature of these people is sufficiently flagrant, this should be done. . . . The emphasis should be on getting desirable people to breed.

THEODORE ROOSEVELT,
"TWISTED EUGENICS"

It is a curious but neglected fact that the very types which in all kindness should be obliterated from the human stock, have been permitted to reproduce themselves and to perpetuate their group, succored by the policy of indiscriminate charity of warm hearts uncontrolled by cool heads.... There is only one reply to a request for a higher birthrate among the intelligent and that is to ask the government to first take the burden of the insane and feebleminded from your back.... Sterilization is the solution.

MARGARET SANGER,
"NEED FOR BIRTH CONTROL IN AMERICA"

It is only by believing in God that we can criticize the Government. Once abolish God, and the Government becomes God. The truth is that irreligion is the opium of the people. Wherever the people do not believe in something beyond the world, they will worship the world. But, above all, they worship the strongest thing in the world.

G. K. CHESTERTON,
CHRISTENDOM IN DUBLIN

Nature is cruel, therefore we too are entitled to be cruel. When I send the flower of German youth into the steel hail of the next war without feeling the slightest regret over the precious German blood that is being spilled, should I not also have the right to eliminate millions of an inferior race that multiplies like vermin?

ADOLF HITLER,
IN JOACHIM FEST, *HITLER*, 1974

There still remains only God to protect Man against Man. Either we will serve him in spirit and in truth or we shall enslave ourselves ceaselessly, more and more, to the monstrous idol we have made with our own hands to our own image and likeness.

ÉTIENNE GILSON,
"THE TERRORS OF THE YEAR TWO THOUSAND"

One who is himself a god needs no religion; he is divine in himself. He must not bow his head. . . . The more man lives in his artificial man-made reality amongst man's structures and machinery, the more strongly he receives the impression that he is the creator of his own existence.

EMIL BRUNNER,
CHRISTIANITY AND CIVILIZATION

Man has always been his own most vexing problem. How shall he think of himself?

REINHOLD NIEBUHR,
THE NATURE AND DESTINY OF MAN

When great causes are on the move in the world . . . we learn that we are spirits and not animals, and that something is going on in space and time, which, whether like it or not, spells "duty."

WINSTON CHURCHILL,
THE UNRELENTING STRUGGLE

Judgment in history falls heaviest on those who come to think themselves gods, who fly in the face of Providence and history, who put their trust in man-made systems and worship the work of their own hands, and who say that the strength of their own right arm gave them the victory.

HERBERT BUTTERFIELD,
CHRISTIANITY AND HISTORY

Man's power over nature is really the power of some men over others with nature as their instrument.

C. S. LEWIS,
THE ABOLITION OF MAN

Philosophy will be unable to effect any immediate change in the current state of the world. This is true not only of philosophy but of all purely human reflection and endeavor. Only a god can save us.

MARTIN HEIDEGGER,
DER SPIEGEL INTERVIEW, 1966

The systems are . . . punishing of any species unwise enough to quarrel with its ecology. Call the systemic forces "God" if you will.

GREGORY BATESON,
STEPS TO AN ECOLOGY OF MIND

Man, from having been one of the many creatures of the planet, has now cast over it his uncontrasted empire. . . . This global human empire possesses the wherewithal to outshine all past civilizations, or it may just as easily end tragically like a colossal Wagnerian Valhalla.

AURELIO PECCEI, FOUNDER OF THE CLUB OF ROME,
THE HUMAN QUALITY

To be men, we must be in control. That is the first and the last ethical word.

JOSEPH FLETCHER,
NEW ENGLAND JOURNAL OF MEDICINE, 1971

We are the children of chaos, and the deep structure of change is decay. At root, there is only corruption, and the unstemmable tide of chaos. Gone is purpose; all that is left is direction. This is the bleakness we have to accept as we peer deeply and dispassionately into the heart of the universe.

PETER ATKINS,
THE SECOND LAW

Is there anything more terrifying than the destruction of the world? Yeah, the knowledge that it doesn't matter one way or the other—that it's all random, radiating aimlessly out of nothing and eventually vanishing forever.

WOODY ALLEN,
SEPTEMBER, 1987

The odds of Homo sapiens surviving the twenty-first century are "no better than fifty-fifty."

MARTIN REES, ASTRONOMER ROYAL,
OUR FINAL CENTURY

The 21st century is an extraordinary time—a century of extremes. We could create much grander civilizations, or we could trigger a new Dark Ages. . . . We're becoming like the sorcerer's apprentice, having started something that we can barely control. In the legend of the sorcerer's apprentice, the apprentice knows the magic is dangerous, but he plays with it anyway when the master is away. He can't resist it. In that story there was a sorcerer and only one apprentice. Now we are all apprentices.

JAMES MARTIN,
THE MEANING OF THE 21ST CENTURY

At the instant the Omega Point is reached, life [Homo sapiens] will have gained control of all matter and forces, not only in a single universe, but in all universes whose existence is logically possible; life will have spread into all spatial regions which could possibly exist.

JOHN BARROW AND FRANK TIPLER,
THE ANTHROPIC COSMOLOGICAL PRINCIPLE

Seventy thousand years ago, Homo sapiens was still an insignificant animal minding its own business in a corner of Africa. In the following millennia it transformed itself into the master of the entire planet and the terror of the ecosystem. Today it stands on the verge of becoming a god, poised to acquire not only eternal youth, but also the divine abilities of creation and destruction. . . .

We are more powerful than ever before, but have very little idea what to do with all that power. Worse still, humans seem to be more irresponsible than ever before. Self-made gods with only the laws of physics to keep us company, we are accountable to no one. We are consequently wreaking havoc on our fellow animals and on the surrounding ecosystem, seeking little more than our own comfort and amusement, yet never finding satisfaction.

Is there anything more dangerous than dissatisfied and irresponsible gods who don't know what they want?

YUVAL NOAH HARARI,
SAPIENS

Long ago, in youth, I was brash enough to think myself able to pronounce on "The Meaning of History." I now know that history's meaning is a matter to be discovered, not declared. . . . Each generation will be judged by whether the greatest, most consequential issues of the human condition have been faced, and that decisions to meet these challenges must be taken by statesmen before it is possible to know what the outcome might be.

HENRY KISSINGER,
WORLD ORDER

Once, after having spoken about some of these ideas someone came up to me and said, "I appreciated your words. But don't you think you are fighting a losing battle?" It was a good question. . . . What I replied, though, was this: "Yes, the Jewish fight is a losing battle. It always was. Moses lost. Joshua lost. Jeremiah lost. We have striven for ideals just beyond our reach, hoped for a gracious society just beyond the possible, believed in a messianic age just over the furthest horizon, wrestled with the angel and emerged limping. And in the meanwhile those who won have disappeared, and we are still here, still young, still full of vigor, still fighting the losing battle, never accepting defeat, refusing to resign ourselves to cynicism, or to give up hope of peace with those who, today as in the past, seek our destruction. That kind of losing battle is worth fighting, more so than any easy victory, any premature consolation."

RABBI JONATHAN SACKS,
FUTURE TENSE

Introduction

Found Faithful

How on earth, it is often asked, could German Christians have caved in so weakly to the allure and coercions of National Socialism in the 1930s? The answer is plain: *All too easily, if you understand the temper of the times in which they lived.* Just so, many Western Christians are caving in weakly before the challenges of our own times, whether through the general seductions and distortions of advanced modernity, the tempting thinking behind the sexual revolution or a failure to understand the significance of the hour and appreciate the implacable hostility of some of the forces against us—and so blunting our witness and betraying the lordship and authority of Jesus. And all this at a time when momentous events across the world are running at a floodtide.

The present stage of history and the character of the advanced modern world have combined to throw down a gauntlet before the church in the West that is as decisive as Rome's demand that Christians offer incense to Caesar as lord. As we shall see, the challenge to the Western church is subtle but unprecedented in its scale, and it must be answered with a courageous *no* to everything that contradicts the call of our Lord—whatever the cost and whatever the outcome. Is Jesus Lord, or are the forces of advanced modernity lord? The church that cannot say *no* to all that contradicts its Lord is a church that is well down the road to cultural defeat and captivity. But the courage to say *no* has to be followed by an equally clear, courageous and constructive *yes*—to the Lord himself, to his gospel and his vision of life, humanity and the future, so that Christians can be seen to live differently and to live better in the world of today.

Christians in the West are living in a grand clarifying moment. The gap between Christians and the wider culture is widening, and many formerly nominal Christians are becoming "religious nones." In many ways we are in the Thursday evening of Holy Week. The cock has not yet crowed, but the angry crowd who would like to see the end of our Lord in the Western world has already seen and heard enough of our early betrayals to believe that it can count on more, and harry us toward ignominious surrender. So this is no time for cowards, for fence sitters or for those who wish to hedge their bets until they hear the judge's verdict on the contest.

We face a solemn hour for humanity at large and a momentous showdown for the Western church. At stake is the attempted completion of the centuries-long assault on the Jewish and Christian faiths and their replacement by progressive secularism as the defining faith of the West and the ideology said to be the best suited to the conditions of advanced modernity. The gathering crisis is therefore about nothing less than a struggle for the soul of the West and the place of faith—any faith—in the life of advanced modern societies. The crisis can be expressed in terms of the interplay of four sets of challenges.

First, the primacy of the Jewish and Christian faiths as the defining faiths of the West has been weakened and almost overcome by two forces: the assault of progressive secularism and the weakening caused by the shaping power of the world of advanced modernity.

Second, within the West itself the near victory of progressive secularism has opened up a further struggle between two post-Christian forces: on one side, nihilism, degeneration and barbarism, which would spell the decline and fall of the West as it falls apart from within; and on the other, the hubris and soaring self-confidence of progressive secularism or evolutionary humanism, which would overreach in trying to lead the West in an entirely new direction and attempting to open up a stunning *new world* for humanity at large.

Third, the overthrow of the Jewish and Christian faiths as the soul of the West has opened the door at the global level to two powerful post-Christian alternatives vying for dominance in the world at large: aggressive secularism and radical Islam.

Fourth, the overall situation raises a double challenge for all the Christian churches across the Western world: Can Christians so witness to their Lord and live out their faith that Christian faith can prevail over the shaping power of the advanced modern world and its institutions? And can Christians, who in some Western countries are still a substantial majority, overcome the militant assaults and ways of life of progressive secularism so as to remain in a position themselves to contribute decisively to the human future?

The major focus of this book is on the challenges of the advanced modern world to the church in the advanced modern world, but they cannot be understood in isolation. Put all these challenges together and take a general's eye view, and the stakes become very clear. For if the anti-Christian forces prevail, they represent nothing less than a return to the philosophy, the ethics and the lifestyles of the pagan world that Christians overcame originally. In other words, today's challenge rivals that of the fateful clash of the early church

with the Caesars in the first three centuries and the menace of the
sultans of Ottoman Islam in the sixteenth.

The details of this grand strategic challenge will unfold as the
argument proceeds, but let me summarize a key part of it in advance: the challenge of advanced modernity is much more than a
matter of ideas. To be sure, Christians in the West are certainly
facing powerful opposition created by the convergence of several
streams of ideas that have created a raging flood that threatens to
overwhelm the Christian faith in its deluge. This flood is the result
of four infamous *S* factors that have built up over several centuries:
Secularism, reinforced by *secularization*, has been empowered by
separationism, and the outcome is a new and formidable form of
statism. (A fifth *S* might be added, the *Sixties*, as there is no question
that in both Europe and America the 1960s had a watershed cultural significance.) Each of these terms and trends are different, and
we will need to define and distinguish them and understand the
connections between them as we go forward. More importantly,
they all need to be resisted with courage and overcome by faith. But
if the forces of advanced modernity have weakened the church,
these other forces are now threatening to complete the overthrow
of the Jewish and Christian faiths as the working faith of the West.

The challenge described here amounts to a grand showdown for
the Western church as a whole. This book is therefore addressed
primarily to Christians throughout the Western world, for they are
in the thick of the crisis. But it is also urgent that Christians and
others outside the West appreciate the strategic global importance
of the crisis of the West and the Western church and their vital part
in responding to it. For one thing, the same challenge is coming to
the rest of the world, for everyone will soon face similar problems
as their own countries and regions modernize. And Western Christians need the help of their sisters and brothers from around the
world, and their contributions to the West may well prove critical.

Sometimes far less numerous in their own countries and usually far less wealthy than Western Christians, Christians in other parts of the world are often better off because they are further behind in terms of modernity. They have not yet become as deeply contaminated by modernity as many Western Christians have been. Like the apostle Peter, they may have less in terms of "silver and gold," but what they have is the faithfulness, the courage, the boldness and the supernatural power that the Western church so often lacks and so badly needs.

In many ways the book is also a quiet tribute to our friends in the Jewish community. As many Jewish leaders have recognized, Jews are facing their own severe crisis today because of defections from Judaism under the conditions of advanced modernity, and this time not primarily because of anti-Semitism or persecution. In the words of Rabbi Jonathan Sacks, "*When it was hard to be a Jew, people stayed Jewish. When it was easy to be a Jew, people stopped being Jewish.* Globally, this is the major Jewish problem of our time."[1]

But while the Jewish crisis is evident, it is also true that we are living in what may be called the Jewish hour. First, more than half the world's inhabitants are followers of one of the three faiths that trace their origins to Abraham. Second, it is time to appreciate the incalculable debt the Western world has long owed to Jewish beliefs and ideas—above all for the gifts of human dignity, freedom and the importance of covenant for political systems that prize freedom. And third, it is time for Christians to appreciate how the secret of the miraculous survival of the Jews in history offers very practical lessons in how Christians are to remain faithful in a post-Christian age. The simple fact is that many of the first things of Judaism are the same first things that many Christians are in danger of forgetting. But they are the very things we must hold fast to if we are to remain faithful to our Lord and demonstrate our own capacity to endure.

All that said, the main focus of this book will be on the American church for several reasons, principally because the United States still represents the world's lead society and therefore experiences the challenges of the advanced modern world in a clearer and sharper way. Importantly too, Christians in America are still a substantial majority, so if they were retored to live as they were called to live, they would have the best chance of living and speaking with integrity—and even helping to prevent the secularist takeover and pointing the world toward a better way.

Yet that compliment is no cause for American complacency, because there are also reasons why the triumph of progressive secularism (or the triumphant return of paganism) could produce more immediate devastation in America than in the rest of the West.

Needless to say, Christians throughout the West often appear to be on the back foot. They have been told repeatedly that their prospects are hopeless. In a thousand withering dismissals we have heard that we are fighting a losing battle and the game is already over. Christians are "yesterday's faith," our day is done, our disagreements with others are a matter of bigotry, and we are reactionaries and on "the wrong side of history." The future is with the faith free, we are told, as if there were such people. The Christianization of Rome and the West was a "false turn" in the long and winding road of history, they say, so the West must return to where it went wrong. The emperor Julian (the "Apostate") may have failed to return Rome to its pagan greatness, but progressive secularists will succeed where Julian failed, though their goal is not to go back, except in their secularist philosophy, but to go forward—forward to the New Frontier or the Promised Land of a new, new world of super-technology, automation, robots, artificial intelligence, guided evolution, Singularity, Omega Point and Omega Man.

We reject such claims simply and completely. On one side, we passionately treasure science, but we equally reject the utopian power fantasies of the scientist-kings who are out to play the role of would-be gods and promote their own much-heralded humanist futures. In the years ahead we humans may explore unimaginable reaches of outer space, but we will still carry with us the crooked timber of our humanity. On the other, we reject the slur that we who are followers of Jesus are either reactionaries or has-beens. As salt and light in today's extraordinary world, our contribution is indispensable. We are not simply guardians of some of the best of the past, but pioneers whose task is to stand against the world for the future of the world—and for the very future of humanity. No less than that is the high calling at stake in many of our present challenges. For serious though our time is, the present challenges are both significant in themselves and harbingers of even weightier ordeals that lie ahead on the horizon. Our responses today are therefore a trial run for the even graver tests that lie ahead, and as the Lord admonished the prophet Jeremiah when he was faint-hearted, "If you have run with footmen and they have tired you out, / Then how can you compete with horses?" (Jer 12:5). Overall, then, a simple question confronts us: If the Christian faith is no longer our own defining and working faith, how do we expect it to remain the defining and working faith of our societies and our civilization?

THE AUDIENCE OF ONE

As followers of Jesus we are called to live before one audience, the audience of One. From Abraham on, the life of faith has always been "all at the sound of a voice." There is only one voice that matters for us—the voice of God, and not the voice of the people or the voice of the times. And certainly not the warm embrace of popularity, the soft whisper of our own desires for comfort, the careful eye to our own reputations, the siren lure of being on the "right side of history," or the mean faces of the bullying activists and the social media mob. Equally, there is only one judgment that matters, and one word of approval that counts in the end: "Well done, good and faithful servant."

My parents tried to teach me that lesson in loyalty when I was a small boy, though there was a long gap between their teaching and my learning it for myself, and there will always be a gap between our knowing what is right and following it faithfully. I grew up in a China that had been ravaged by two centuries of European and American adventuring, and then by World War II and a brutal civil war. We lived in Nanjing, which was then the nation's capital, but there were few good schools to go to, so at the age of five I found myself setting off by plane to a boarding school in Shanghai.

Obviously, the conditions behind the decision to send me out at that age were extreme, and I was not the only one launched on that path so young. But it was the first time in my life that I had been away from my parents and on my own. So, to give me a constant reminder of the North Star of the faith at the center of our family life, my father had searched for two small, smooth, flat stones and painted on them his life motto and that of my mother. For many years those two little stones were tangible memos in the pockets of my gray flannel shorts that were the uniform of most English schoolboys in those days. In my right-hand pocket was my father's motto, "Found Faithful," and in my left-hand pocket was my mother's, "Please Him."

Many years have passed since then, and both of those little painted stones were lost in the chaos of escaping from China when Mao Zedong and the People's Army eventually overran Nanjing, returned the capital to Beijing and began their iron and bloody rule of the entire country. But I have never forgotten the lesson of the little stones. Followers of Jesus are called to be "found faithful" and to "please him," always, everywhere and in spite of everyone and everything.

That same faithfulness braced our Christian brothers and sisters in China as they took the full brunt of one of the most vicious, cruel and systematic persecutions in all history. And as I write now, we are witnessing almost daily the same astonishing courage of Christians in many countries of the world, but especially in the Islamic Middle East that was once the cradle of the church. Day after day Christians are standing as martyrs, facing false charges, assaults, mutilation, rape, religious cleansing, murder, bomb blasts, beheadings and even crucifixions, all because they will not renounce the name of Jesus.

And what of us in the West? Are we showing that we too are prepared to follow Jesus and his authority at any cost? When an imperceptible bow would have saved Daniel's three friends, they defied King Nebuchadnezzar's idolatry at the threat of being burned alive. When simply closing a window and drawing his curtains could have saved Daniel himself, he chose to risk the lions rather than mute his allegiance to God. When a mere whiff of incense would have saved their lives, early Christians refused to acknowledge Caesar as lord rather than Jesus and were made human torches or the evening meal for wild animals. When it seemed quixotic to take on the emperor, the empress and all the empire, Athanasius took his stand for truth *contra mundum* (against the world) and was exiled five times for his faithfulness. When he was told he was arrogant or out of his mind to follow his conscience and defy the consensus of tradition, Martin Luther stood firm in the face of the fiery stake that had cremated Jan Hus before him. When his closest friends urged him to save himself for the important work of his future scholarship, Dietrich Bonhoeffer chose to reenter Hitler's lair and ignore the looming specter of the gallows.

What then of us? Are we living in the light of the great cloud of witnesses and martyrs who have gone before us? Or in the comfortable conditions of the advanced modern world, where the seductions of modernity are more of a threat to our faithfulness than persecution? In the golden era of the Roman Empire, Pliny the Younger advised Emperor Trajan that Christians should be executed solely for their tenacity and intransigence. "Whatever the nature of their admission, I am convinced that their stubbornness and unshakable obstinacy ought not to go unpunished."[2] The similar charge in the death of many martyrs was routine: "Since they remained unbending, obstinate, I have condemned them."[3]

Would we be convicted today for being stubborn, tenacious, unbending and obstinate? It is surely undeniable that only rarely in Christian history has the lordship of Jesus in the West been treated as more pliable or has Christian revisionism been more brazen, Christian interpretations of the Bible more self-serving, Christian preaching more soft, Christian behavior more lax, Christian compromise more common, Christian defections from the faith more casual, and Christian rationales for such slippage more spurious and shameless.

Let me say it again: How on earth could German Christians have caved in so weakly to the allure and coercions of National Socialism in the 1930s? The answer is plain: *All too easily, if you understand the temper of the times in which they lived.* Just so, many Western Christians are caving in weakly before the challenges of our own times, such as the general seductions and distortions of modernity, the particular temptations of the sexual revolution or a failure to appreciate the implacable hostility of the forces against us—and so blunting our witness and denying the lordship of Jesus and the authority of the Scriptures. It is time, and past time, to turn this situation around and take a stand worthy of our Lord—before the cock crows and we are left with the bitter regret that our brothers and sisters around the world stood firm and paid with their lives, but our generation in the West betrayed our Lord in such a pitiful way.

UNCLUBBABLE

Why "impossible people"? The term *impossible man* was used to describe the eleventh-century Benedictine reformer Peter Damian (c. 1007–1073). Dante placed Damian in the highest circle of paradise as a saint and the predecessor of Francis of Assisi. A thousand years ago, as in our own time, there was little regard for truth or for the integrity and purity of the Christian faith. Nor was there much sense of the gravity of sin, so the church was easygoing, corruption was rife and the moral and theological rot was as pervasive among the clergy and the leaders of the church as among ordinary people. (As in the times of the Hebrew prophets, so among Evangelicals today, it is too often the pastors, the shepherds, who are leading the people astray—though *celebrity shepherds* is surely a contradiction in terms.) Above all, Damian called for reform against the most prominent evils. In particular, he attacked the widespread practice of simony, the selling of church positions for money, and the equally widespread acceptance of homosexuality, pedophilia and pederasty, especially among the clergy.

In recognition of his reforming fervor, Damian was later canonized by the Catholic Church as St. Peter Damian. Criticized in his time for being fanatical and purely negative, he was in fact passionate about the church's "welfare of souls" and about faithfulness to Jesus and the truth of the gospel. Yet it was these positive passions that made him severe and unsparing in his denunciation of all forms of corruption and immorality, and in attacking them he could not be swayed by either obstacles or opposition. His commitment to Jesus alone was so fierce that he won the reputation for being *unmanipulable, unbribable, undeterrable* and, in George Orwell's later term of approval, *unclubbable* ("clubbable" being the ultimate in coercion through comfortable conformity).

Unquestionably, the term *impossible man* was ambiguous. It could be taken either as a compliment or an insult. Doubtless, many of Peter Damian's generation admired him for his stand, just as many hated him for his fervor, and many were frustrated and made uncomfortable by what they saw as his intransigence. In other words, the same term could express either admiration or exasperation, as it will again today. But all that was irrelevant to Peter Damian. He spoke, wrote and acted solely with an eye to the audience of One. He could not be deterred by other voices. He was faithful to Jesus alone and above all. His faith had a backbone of steel. He was the impossible man.

It would be tempting to underscore that we especially need Christian leaders like that. The story is told that a Roman praetorian prefect was so offended by St. Basil's outspoken statements that he declared that he had never been addressed like that in his life. "No doubt," St. Basil replied, "you have never met a bishop." (Clearly he was speaking in a day when bishops were not yet political appointees and to be a bishop was not what it became: a position with the promise of power and personal advancement. The church will never be free so long as we continue to have that kind of bishop appointed for reasons other than churchly). But the challenge today goes far wider than leaders. All who would be faithful followers of Jesus in our advanced modern world are facing similar challenges and seductions, and we too must become impossible people—Christians with hearts that can melt with compassion, but with faces like flint and backbones of steel who are unmanipulable, unbribable, undeterrable and unclubbable, without ever losing the gentleness, the mercy, the grace and the compassion of our Lord. Whether we are Evangelicals, Catholics, Orthodox or Pentecostals, we must have a rock solid allegiance to Jesus alone, above all and despite everyone and everything. "Jesus is Lord" is our allegiance, our confession, our authority and our standard and rule of life. Whoever and whatever contradicts him summons us again to count the cost and to take our stand. Christians today need to be broad-shouldered—made so by carrying the weight of the cross as we were commanded.

Impossible People is a companion to my earlier book *Renaissance*, which came first for a reason. In that book I explored the reasons for our response of assured faith in the gospel—which must be forever unshakeable—and it concluded with hope. I deliberately reversed the normal order of "challenge and response" and put the response before the challenge. Such is the character and record of the gospel of Jesus that we may trust it absolutely however dark the times and however bleak the challenge. Doom, gloom, alarmism and fear are never the way for the people of God. We are to have "no fear." *Impossible People* addresses the challenges we face and subjective side that is our response to these challenges—the gospel carries its own inherent transforming power, but we need to trust it, obey it and live it—against all the odds and at any cost. We need to respond to the gospel with courage and conviction, in order to live faithfully according to the call of Jesus and the good news of his kingdom in today's world.

We need never have qualms about the objective side of the challenge. The gospel of Jesus may be trusted to be the transforming power that it is. It is, after all, the very power of God for the saving of humanity, and the record of its impact in history is glorious and undeniable. Our allegiance to it is the concern today. We have to rise to the challenge that the gospel raises to all who say that they believe it—we must demonstrate our confidence in the gospel by a courage that is prepared to break with all that contradicts with what God says. In short, by faith we must be prepared to wager our comfort, our livelihood, our honor and our very lives on God and his Word against all other claims and authorities. We must therefore live as we have been called to live: to take up our crosses and to count the cost of living lives that are true to the gospel and to the lordship of Jesus, regardless of the cost and the consequences in our day—and so be worthy of the great cloud of witnesses behind us in history and around us in the world today.

One of the greatest Christian leaders of the last century was John R. W. Stott, rector of All Souls Langham Place in London and a peerless preacher, Bible teacher, evangelist, author, global leader and friend to many. I knew him over many decades, but I will never forget my last visit to his bedside three weeks before he died. After an unforgettable hour and more of sharing many memories over many years, I asked him how he would like me to pray for him. Lying weakly on his back and barely able to speak, he answered in a hoarse whisper, "Pray that I will be faithful to Jesus until my last breath."

Would that such a prayer be the passion of our generation too. The Jewish sages point out that when Moses pleaded with God to forgive the people for their rebellion over the golden calf, he cited the very reason God had given for deciding to abandon them. ("It is a stiff-necked people.") Did Moses not see the illogic of what he was asking? But that of course was the very point of his request. The same stubbornness that was the Jews' worst vice at Sinai would one day be their noblest virtue when tempted to abandon their faith in God. Only such a stiff-necked stubbornness would enable the Jews to resist the threat of death and the seduction of conversion to another faith.

The church of Jesus can never be the church without both faith and faithfulness, and both of them in a form that is strong to the point of being stubborn. The supreme challenge of the hour for the church of Jesus in the advanced modern world is to so live and speak as witnesses to our Lord that, as in the motto of the US Marines, we are "Semper Fi"—always *Found Faithful*. Rarely in two thousand years of Christian history has that calling been so tested as it is in our time. Come threats of death or seductive temptations to an easy life, our task is to stand faithful to our Lord in every moment of our lives and faithful to our last breath.

➣ A Prayer ⩣

O LORD OUR GOD, you are the one true God, beside whom there is no other. In you alone lies our trust, our salvation and our hope. We do not trust ourselves, we cannot save ourselves, and our hope is not in ourselves. To stake our existence in the vastness of the cosmos anywhere other than in you is folly, and to seek for strength and wisdom apart from you in the hazardous journey of life is madness. Be to us, small and sinful though we are, all that you can be, so that, brought to life by your grace, strengthened by your power and warmed by your love, we may trust you with our whole hearts as your faithfulness and covenant loyalty so richly deserve. Through Jesus Christ our Lord, Amen.

QUESTIONS FOR DISCUSSION

1. Discuss the nub of the claims about what is at stake for the Western church today, and why this is critical for Christians throughout the rest of the world. What would you add to the picture, and what would you change?

2. Why do you think Christians have become so culturally weak when they remain a sizable community in terms of numbers?

3. What is meant by a faithfulness that is "unclubbable"? Where do you see examples of Christians being "comfortable conformists"? Is this simply pious rhetoric, or does it have wider implications for the way we live?

chapter one

New World, Old Challenge

One of my most memorable return visits to China as an adult included the privilege of addressing a forum of Chinese CEOs in the business school of one of China's most prestigious universities. It was an official occasion, and there was a lengthy program that included the singing of the Communist Party anthem and the cutting of a gigantic birthday cake for the Party. But after all that had gone on before I spoke, I was surprised at the intensity with which people listened and then engaged in a spirited discussion about the state of the world. But the most searching question of the day was raised at the end by the dean of the business school as we walked back to the lecture hall from the closing dinner.

"Allow me to ask a question I didn't want to ask in public," the dean said to me. "What am I missing? We in China are fascinated by the Christian roots of the Western past in order to see what we can learn for the sake of China's future. But you in the West are cutting yourself off from your roots. What am I missing? And what happens if this continues?"

Sadly, I had to say to the dean that he was missing nothing, and the consequences for the West would be momentous. The West is cutting off its Jewish and Christian roots and destroying the entire root system of its culture, but dire though that is for the West, it cannot be viewed in isolation. It needs to be viewed from a wider-angled perspective. The future of the world in the next generations will be shaped decisively by the answer to three great questions, all of which are inescapably religious, and one of which concerns his question directly.

1. Will Islam modernize peacefully in the end? (The crux of the issue turns on the question of whether Muslims will accept freedom of conscience for all whose beliefs differ from them and therefore shift their approach to others from conflict and coercion to persuasion.)

2. Which faith or ideology will replace Marxism in China? (While the Communist party is in power, the ideology is dead, and the question is its replacement. Will it be nationalism, materialism, Confucianism, Buddhism or the Christian faith?)

3. Will the Western world sever or recover its roots? (The subject of this book.)

Simple-sounding at first, there is far more to each of those questions than meets the eye. The dean's interest, and mine here too, concerns the response to the third question. The attempted overthrow of the Jewish and Christian faiths by progressive secularism means that the Western world has gone a long way down the road in the process of cutting off its cultural roots, so that the Jewish and Christian faiths have lost their dominant place as the prime shapers of Western civilization. It is often said that the fourth century AD was the long transition period when the Christian faith took over from paganism as the dominant faith of the West—and therefore that our own time is the hinge period for a grand reversion. Put differently, where Julian the Apostate failed in his attempt to stem the Christian advance and restore paganism, many modern secularists are openly attempting to reverse the process and return to a different outcome.

Any secularist claims of "mission accomplished" would be premature and a matter of wishful thinking. We are still in the interim period, the contest is far from over, and most people have yet to face up to the consequences of destroying the Jewish and Christian root system. Quite obviously, the culture war is far from Platonic, and it is raging still. But to mix my metaphors, the West is seeking to do the near impossible: to cross the river while changing horses in mid-stream and still maintain its greatness. But the inescapable effect is that what greatness remains in the West today is that of a cut-flower civilization. The West has lost its soul. It is no longer distinguished and admired for its ideals it once had, for these have either vanished or are viewed only as the spurious claims of a hypocrite. Increasingly now, if the West is admired, it is only for its technological prowess, its economic prosperity and its military power, all of which will soon fade too. Yet while the West is no longer Christian in its foundations, it is not yet fully non-Christian (secularist or pagan) either, though its post-Christian phase may soon reach the point of no return.

Different countries in the West show their characteristic differences over the place of the severed cultural roots, and there are significant differences between Protestant countries and Catholic countries, as well as between Europe and the United States as a whole. But the roots are being severed decisively almost everywhere, and the determined attempt to shift foundations is underway. But we can say with an organic certainty, which is as sure as any mathematical certainty, that the growth and the flowers that they once produced will eventually die.

Cut-flower civilization? The destruction of a root system and a moral ecology? A civilization without a soul? We could give more sophisticated names to this crisis. We might call it a "legitimation crisis" or a "crisis of cultural authority" in that the beliefs and ideas that once inspired and drove the West have been repudiated and have almost lost their compelling power. We might also trace the outcomes in which the problem is working itself out in Western societies now, for another way to view the cut-flower civilization is to recognize the yawning vacuum at the heart of our societies, hollowed out by the convergence of three trends.

First, there has been a direct repudiation of the once powerful Jewish and Christian beliefs that formed the foundations of the Western world and its key ideas and ideals. This is partly due to the all-out attack of philosophies such as secularism, partly due to the global explosion of pluralism that commonly collapses into relativism, and partly due (as we shall see later) to the manner in which advanced modernity minimizes and marginalizes all values other than its own. The result is nothing less than the dysfounding of the West and a fracturing of the former Jewish and Christian consensus, and its outcome is a chaotic conflict of voices in a grand conflict of "Says who?" In many circles that regard themselves as the cultural elite, it is now taken for granted that secularism and its naturalistic worldview is self-evident, whereas Jewish and Christian views are passé, uncouth, reactionary and nothing but a barrier to what is now seen as human flourishing and progress.

Second, there has been a subtle shift in the meaning of many Western ideas, so that once-strong Jewish and Christian terms are now used in different ways that decisively change their meaning and sustainability. *Freedom*, for example, has been gutted of its solid Jewish and Christian understanding, and in its contemporary loosely libertarian and libertine forms is highly appealing but quite unsustainable. Yet the shift and the substitution have taken place so slowly and subtly that few have even noticed, and most live blithely on as if all were as before.

And third, the attempt to sustain the Jewish and Christian ideas and ideals by directly transposing them into a secularist key can increasingly be seen as a failure. The blunt truth is that secularism and other alternative philosophies that claim to replace the Jewish and Christian roots have no adequate root system of their own with which to nourish the ideals. Witness, for example, the inability of the new atheists to provide an adequate foundation for such notions as the sanctity of life, the dignity of the individual person, the responsibility of freedom, justice, equality and universality—let alone any antidote to the mounting inequalities and polarizations in society. Once rooted in the belief that every last human is precious and has an inalienable dignity because he or she is made in the image of God, and that freedom is the gift through which humans most resemble their Creator, such biblical roots have been cut and their fruits are withering.

In each of these three sources of the vacuum we can confidently speak of the Jewish and Christian roots, for there is undeniable truth in Benjamin Disraeli's observation that the Christian faith is "Judaism for the multitudes." Or George Eliot's comment that Jewish "ideas have determined the religion of half the world, and that, the more cultivated half."[1] As Jonathan Sacks points out, one of the key differences between the outcomes of the English and American revolutions and the French and Russian revolutions was that the political philosophy of the former was grounded in the thinking of the Puritans, who in fact were "Christian Hebraists who based their thought on the history of ancient Israel."[2]

Among the numerous consequences of these trends, the default position now adopted by many Western intellectuals has created our "ABC moment" (Anything but Christianity). Any weird, wild and wonderful idea can be espoused, and often is—so long as it is not Jewish and Christian. This dismissal takes different forms in different countries, but it can be witnessed almost everywhere throughout the West. A British cabinet minister recently described the absurd outcome in Britain, a country with undeniable Christian roots that were once acknowledged and appreciated.

If we're Roman Catholics, we're accessories to child abuse. If we're Anglo-Catholics, we're homophobic bigots curiously attached to velvet and lace, if we're liberal Anglicans, we're pointless hand-wring conscience-hawkers, and if we're Evangelicals we're creepy obsessives who are uncomfortable with anyone enjoying anything more louche than a slice of Battenberg [a light sponge cake covered in marzipan]. Even in an area where Christianity might be supposed to be vaguely relevant—moral reasoning—it's casually assumed that Christian belief is an actively disabling factor.[3]

Sadly, the Jewish community is not immune to the crisis, and this time the crisis cannot be blamed on anti-Semitism. There may not be the same public gloating over Jewish decline as there is over the statistics of Christian decline, but the reality for the Jews in the West is even worse than for Christians. On the one hand, defections from the Jewish faith are at an all-time high. In the words of Rabbi Sacks,

> Today throughout the Diaspora one Jew in two is either marrying out, or not marrying, or in some other way deciding not to create a Jewish home, have Jewish children and continue the Jewish story. . . .
>
> The Jewish community in the United States, the largest in the world, is disappearing faster than any other since the Lost Ten Tribes vanished from the pages of history more than two and a half thousand years ago. The same thing is happening, slightly less dramatically, in Britain. . . . The Jewish community has lost ten Jews a day every day, for more than ten years.[4]

On the other hand, Sacks stresses that the Western assaults on the Christian faith are also an assault on the core ideals of Judaism. "The liberal democracies of the West are abandoning the very values that were once known as the Judeo-Christian tradition. . . . Society is not becoming more Jewish but manifestly and rapidly less so."[5]

Western Christians cannot close their eyes to this state of affairs. It would be hard to do so even if we wished to. But we must not use it as an excuse for nostalgia, for playing the victim card or for fighting back like the apostle Peter, who mistakenly thought the kingdom of God could be defended with a sword and then betrayed his Master by falling silent rather than speaking when the going became dangerous. Machiavelli rightly described Jesus as "the unarmed prophet," especially in contrast to Muhammad. Jesus plainly vetoed certain responses that are false and dangerous because his kingdom is a different kind of kingdom, and he warned his followers bluntly how we should expect to be treated if we are faithful to him. And of course our fellow Christians in other parts of the world are facing attacks far worse than we are—persecution rather than discrimination and death rather than derision.

But far more serious than our new cultural discomfort is the dangerous vacuum created at the heart of our Western civilization. The cut-flower condition creates a vacuum of ideas and ideals that cannot continue forever. Indeed, as we shall see, it has created the conditions for the rise of the titanic struggle mentioned earlier—between the forces of decadence and chaos on one side and the forces of hubris and overweening self-confidence on the other. If allowed to expand unchecked, these forces will destroy the West from within, and the West will no longer be a distinctive civilization but merely a geographical designation on the map. As I said, the West is still *post*-Christian rather than *non*-Christian, but the crisis is well advanced and the difference between the two terms is harder and harder to distinguish.

There is no better window into the momentous clash between the Jewish and Christian faiths as the foundation of the West and the progressive secularism of those who wish to replace them than

the ten televised debates in 1968 between William F. Buckley and
Gore Vidal. Brilliantly captured in the documentary *The Best of
Enemies*, the film pits two eloquent American patricians who were
united in class, in Ivy League education and in their command of
debating skills, but bitterly divided in philosophy, ethics and goals.
On one side was Buckley, the Catholic whose book *God and Man
at Yale* and whose magazine *The National Review* had ignited the
modern conservative revolution and accelerated the election of
Ronald Reagan. And on the other was Vidal, a precocious and pro-
lific writer, *enfant terrible* of the political left, one of the first publicly open homosexuals and an apostle of the sexual revolution. The
loathing between the two men was palpable and the result was
more carnival and circus than reasoned debate. The climax came
in the ninth debate in a moment of explosive anger when Vidal
smirked and accused Buckley of being a "crypto-Nazi." Buckley
blasted back, "Now listen, you queer. Stop calling me a crypto-Nazi
or I'll sock you in your g_____ face and you'll stay plastered."

When Buckley lost his cool, Vidal was widely judged to have won
the debate, but the enduring feud between the two men mattered
less than its cultural significance. It revealed the divide that even
then was beginning to blaze out into the American culture war.
1968 was the *annus calamitosus* of the 1960s. It was the year of
student unrest, turmoil over the My Lai massacre and the Vietnam
War, the Black Power salute at the Olympics, the assassinations of
Martin Luther King Jr. and Bobby Kennedy, and the second series
of the debates took place during the riots at the Democratic Convention in Chicago. *Time* magazine's Lance Morrow wrote that
"Like a knife blade, the year severed past from future."[6] And col-
umnist George Will called 1968 "perhaps the worst year in American
history."[7] Needless to say, the debates themselves were not decisive
in causing the vast chasm, but they revealed it with unmistakable
clarity. For the discerning, they were the plain, blunt statement of

the intense struggle between the two faiths that were fighting to the death to define the soul of America—and the West.

Such a comment raises a cluster of questions, such as why and how this crisis developed. But my concern is our response today rather than analysis. The truth is that the world, as Christians have known it for many centuries, has gone—and gone for good. We are confronting a new situation. The explosion of pluralism alone makes ours a situation that has not been seen since the diversity of the Roman Empire. So we have to face up not just to others rejecting us but to all that is new in the grand transformations in human experience that are shaping our lives in the early twenty-first century. Many of the changes we are seeing have been underway for several centuries, so there is no simple baseline for claiming that a Jewish and Christian consensus was once largely intact in the West. But in the English-speaking world we might loosely take the 1950s as the most recent decade in which there was some semblance of a Jewish and Christian consensus that still retained much of its former cultural strength.

Now, just a few decades later, it is plain that any such consensus has gone so decisively that any simple return or reclamation is out of the question. That is one reason, among several, why much of the recent Christian culture warring has been in vain. The recognizably Christian world that Christians helped to create and that has been dominant in the West for more than a thousand years has severely eroded, rival faiths (supremely secularism) are growing in both numbers and power, their damaging influence has spread far beyond their own circles, and the future we are all facing together is in some ways radically new for us all as human beings. We therefore have to begin by assessing the transformations of our world, and the way they are shaping human experience in novel ways, and then consider what Christian faithfulness means in the light of these new realities, realities that before long will also shape

the future of our fellow believers in all other parts of the world. I
will outline some of the directly spiritual challenges in later chapters,
but let's begin with some of the grand global transformations and
their significance for our generation.

FROM PYROTECHNOLOGY TO BIOTECHNOLOGY

The first grand transformation is foundational, but far less discussed
than it should be. It is important because it concerns the way in
which we humans see ourselves and our place in the universe, and
how we relate to the world of nature in which we live as the leading
creatures in our little blue ball of a planet home. Our human world
is shifting, it is said, from the "age of pyrotechnology," based on the
engineering of fire, to the "age of biotechnology," based on the engineering of life.[8] Seen from our present perspective, the Industrial
Revolution was epochal and both radical and profoundly disruptive,
though it was powerfully innovative and a potent thrust forward in
human progress. The infamous political revolutions and the global
world wars that it spawned, supremely Russian communism,
German fascism and World Wars I and II, were titanic and destructive. But in fact they were simply partial expressions of the
multiple revolutions in human experience that came in the wake of
industrialization—and the technological and social revolutions
have been even more revolutionary and lasting than the political
and military.

The Industrial Revolution began in England in the eighteenth
century with the invention of machines such as the steam engine
and the weaver's loom, and it bulldozed its path throughout the
Western world, dislocating us from the past and hurtling us
forward as it advanced. As it did so, industrialization represented
a giant leap forward for humankind, shifting humanity from
agrarian societies to industrial societies, from the natural world to
the mechanical world, from the countryside to the city, and thus,

in Jeremy Rifkin's words, from the "world of haystacks" to the "world of smoke stacks."[9]

The revolutionary significance of the industrial era should not be minimized. Yet it must be seen not only as the dawn of a new era *but as the end of an old one*. For seen from a longer historical perspective the Industrial Revolution was the final phase in the long history of pyrotechnology that stretches back thousands of years into the long past. From this perspective pyrotechnology was itself once revolutionary, for in its day it meant an equally titanic shift from the *power of human muscles* to the *power of fire*. Thinkers from Plato to Lewis Mumford to Jeremy Rifkin and Yuval Harari have all in their turn underscored the importance of fire and the long eras in history that were made possible by the use of fire.

Until the harnessing of fire, it is said, the strength and significance of all the earth's animals depended on the strength of their bodies—"the strength of their muscles, the size of their teeth, the breadth of their wings. Though they may harness winds and currents, they are unable to control these natural forces, and are always constrained by their physical design."[10] But when humans gained control of fire, they took a gigantic leap forward.

When Prometheus stole fire from the gods, Plato noted, it gave humans a source of knowledge and power that once belonged to the gods alone. It was fire above all, Mumford argued, that gave us the three gifts of light, power and heat, which allowed humans to triumph over nature and build our "second nature," our own technologically built human world over against the world of nature we once lived in. With the rise of the age of fire, Rifkin writes, the "pounding, squeezing, breaking, mashing and grinding" of human muscle power "began to play second fiddle to fusing, melting, soldering, forging and burning" made possible by fire.[11] Through the engineering made possible by the arts of fire, including the use of the stored-up energy of the sun in the form of fossil fuels, humanity has been able to build its own "second home" independent of the world of nature and drive its progress forward with a prodigious, Promethean energy.

The grand age of pyrotechnology, however, is ending. Its close is partly due to the foreseeable exhaustion of nonrenewable energy and the alarms raised by damage to the earth and the accelerating extinction of the animal species in the industrial era. But it is due even more to the rise of a new kind of human engineering—the engineering of life forms. This is the revolutionary significance of biotechnology. Beginning in the twentieth century with discoveries in biology and genetics, but long foretold in such myths as the *golem* of Jewish tradition, the Greek story of Icarus and his wax wings, Goethe's "Sorcerer's Apprentice," Mary Shelley's *Franken-stein* and Friedrich Nietzsche's "The Master and His Emissary," humanity is now setting out to engineer forms of life itself.

The biogenetic revolution is still in its earliest moments, and many of the predictions of the posthuman future are in the realm of science fiction conjectures, though written by serious scientists. But as with the wholesale engineering of fire, the significance of biogenetics for humanity is stunning in its potential. Plato's philosopher-kings have given way to our modern scientist-kings, and belief in God as Creator has been replaced by confidence in Man as Creator. Instead of working on external forms of nature, we are now on the verge of being able to transform, and to combine in new forms, the very nature of life itself—and from the inside. ("We can now engineer the human race," the *MIT Technology Review* tells us modestly. They have a lab in which "man rebuilds creation to suit himself.")[12] And as ever, regardless of the risks, the unforeseen consequences and the unknown aftermaths, we can be certain that "if it can be done, it will be done," and that "if we (say, in the West) don't do it, someone else (in Russia, China, Iran or India) will."

My interest is not in a history lesson but in the spiritual and moral significance of this new leap forward. All who have read the story of the Tower of Babel in Genesis 11 will appreciate the spiritual importance of what the fired-mud bricks made possible for the Sumerians in their time. With their kilns, their bricks, their hard glazed ceramics, their stunning art and their soaring super-ziggurats, (along with the invention of the wheel, the arch and the calendar) people in the region of Babylon had the building materials to make a name for themselves by themselves, and so become as God. Their manmade "holy mountains" would span the chasm between heaven and earth, God and humanity. The Lord himself recognized this fact—"And now nothing which they purpose to do will be impossible for them" (Gen 11:6). Humans could harness technology to give heft to their dream of being like God himself and therefore of not needing God at all. Our scientist-kings and our brave new age of biotechnology (and then astrotechnology: the engineering of space) are the latest in giant steps that will take this Babel drive to a new level.

At the spiritual level it carries with it the greatest boost to the pretensions of human autonomy and idolatry since Babel and takes it far beyond such disastrous stumbles as the fiasco of Stalin's "new man" and Hitler's "new race." At the moral level, as we shall see later, it will be ushered in with genuine and marvelous breakthroughs in the battle against hereditary weakness and disease. But it will also resurrect the specter of new and refined forms of eugenics that could make the appalling Nazi experiments and China's horrendous gendercide policy look primitive. As contemporary initiatives demonstrate, such as the Singularity Project (with its goal of "digital immortality") and the Gilgamesh Project (with its goal of overcoming death), the grand shift from pyrotechnology to biotechnology (and then astrotechnology) is a transformation of the utmost spiritual and cultural significance and far more important than the present level of the discussion suggests. As philosopher Mary

Midgeley warns, what we are seeing in the power fantasies of the future from the new scientist-kings is nothing less than "the promotion of human minds to the honor of retrospectively creating the cosmos."[13] What they are offering is "an endless evolutionary escalator exalting the human race" and ushering in "the apotheosis of Man."[14] Soaring on the strength of its titanic triumphs, such as the Manhattan Project and the Apollo moon landing, science is now hailed as omnicompetent and omniscient, with its promise of a Theory of Everything. Scientific man in his neo-Babel form is now "as God himself." In creating humanity with its capacity for freedom, God took the risk of creating a form of life that could defy him, but that risk and that defiance has reached the level at which humanity, in its attempt to be as God himself, now has the power to destroy itself and creation. In the extravagant comment of physicist Paul Davies, "Truly, we should be lords of the universe."[15]

The Jewish sages have long reminded us that the two key words in the story of Babel, *bricks* and *confuse*, are a precise inversion of each other in Hebrew. In the hubris of their attempt to "make a name for themselves" and erase the very boundaries between "heaven" and "earth," the builders of Babel became the everlasting symbol of confusion and showed that their civilization was all too human in its turn. Just so do human intentions always carry the seeds of unintended consequences. Just so do utopian dreams always become nightmares, whether those dreams are ancient Babylonian, recent Marxist or Western secularist in the future.

THE INDUSTRIAL AGE TO THE INFORMATION AGE

The second grand transformation is equally vital because it concerns the way in which we humans are aware of each other, relate to each other through our communications and are capable of responding to our greatest human challenges. We are shifting, it is said again, from the industrial age to the information age—through globalization. If the first transformation is discussed less than it should be, this second one is far more obvious and discussed endlessly, so much so that it is easy to dismiss it as trendy nonsense or "globaloney." To be sure, we always have to make claims about globalization with care, for we need to recognize important earlier phases of globalization, and any description must always include its countervailing trends. As the trade jargon puts it, the global world is "globalizing," "localizing" and even "glocalizing" at the same time.

All that said, there is no question that globalization is real and of momentous significance. It can be defined accurately as *the process by which human interconnectedness is reaching a genuinely global level.* Market capitalism is an obvious leader of the forces exploiting the new global potential, but globalization should not be limited to economics. The real driver is information technology—and in particular the speed, scale and simultaneity of information technology in the age of the computer and the Internet—or the "triple screen effect" of living nearly half of our daily lives before the modern trinity of the television screen, the computer screen and the screen on our mobile phone or handheld devices.

Descriptions of globalization are often abstract, but the reality hits our daily lives in ways that are far more concrete. The impact can be captured in the plethora of slogans bandied around today to describe the novelty of the global era: "Everyone is now everywhere." "With our instant, total information, we are the first generation to see everything as it happens." "Everything is interconnected and no one is in charge." "You can reach anywhere in the world from anywhere else, and in twenty-four hours." "We live in a global village," but in many ways the world is not smaller but larger, because "in the interconnected world today's leaders have to be in touch with the whole world the whole time." And so on and so on.

What matters supremely is that globalization is a revolution in human knowing and thinking. All technological advances are revolutionary in some way, but many affect only the way we do things. But revolutions in human knowing are the most revolutionary of all because they shape the way we think—for example, the titanic impact of earlier revolutions such as the invention of writing, the alphabet and printing. Through its speed, globalization makes thinking and knowledge instantaneous; through its scope and scale it makes knowledge unprecedented in volume; and through its simultaneity it makes knowledge attainable by all and therefore a mass phenomenon.

Once again, what matters here is neither the history nor the exact process through which we have reached this point, but the consequences. And in the case of globalization they are myriad and they are momentous. It would be possible to trace the consequences in a broad range of areas, from human identity to the family, to community, to work, to consumerism, to politics, to international relations and numerous other areas. But let me take two consequences that are crucial to the integrity and effectiveness of faith in the advanced modern world. One is the impact of globalization on our sense of time and the other its impact on the magnification of world problems such as evil and suffering.

TIME BOUND, TIME TORN

As humans, we are both time bound and "time torn" (Thomas Hardy). We always have been, and we always will be. Time's arrow flies through history fast and unstoppably. Our lives are embedded in time just as fish swim in water, and they are limited by time like the products in our supermarkets with their sell-by dates. But with the invention of the clock in thirteenth-century Europe, we have slowly grown bound and torn by time in a new way. We no longer live by the rhythms of nature and the seasons, but by the clock. Our time is always "o'clock" or "of the clock." With industrialization in the nineteenth century, typified by spreading railway networks that ran according to their thickening railway timetables, such features as speed, precision, coordination and efficiency became prominent features of our early modern awareness of time.

That, however, was then, and for all its advances, industrial time was still primitive—for in the global era we have now advanced to the world of the truly instant and immediate and seemingly obliterated the stubborn reality of space. No human need toil, no horse need run, no sail need be hoisted and no engines need to be fired and stoked, for what we wish to say and anything we wish to send is there before we know it—and all effortlessly at the touch of a button or a computer key.

To be sure, the result is a world of instant gratification and a thousand effortless conveniences that are all to our good. But it is also a world of constant overload. We may have conquered space and shrunk geography, straddling the world in hours rather than days, weeks or months, but we have not conquered time, and our time saving has turned into our time slaving. Yes, in our travel and our communications we have vanquished the gap between here and there and between now and then. But in our restless haste we have also obliterated the gap between one thing and the next thing so that our breaking news, our emails, our phone calls, our texts and our to-do lists come faster and more crowded than ever. (At a dinner not long ago, my wife's host received more than five hundred emails between his saying grace and finishing dessert.)

So our vaunted human triumph over time has been pyrrhic. We now live in a world of "speed, stuff and stress" and under the relentless tyranny of the "urgent now." The boundaries between work and leisure, public and private, are dissolving, so that we have no rest and we are all forced to be time jugglers and multitaskers. We are all rats in the rat race. We are all overwhelmed by all we have to do, and we struggle with priorities to remember and agendas to keep under control. Time slaves under an unforgiving master, we are all Darwinians now, living under the daily threat of "the survival of the fastest."

So who then has time to think? To think for ourselves rather than taking the Internet consensus as fast food for the mind? To think sufficiently in the light of biblical wisdom to be able to be discerning? To have the space for worship, for solitude, for the spiritual disciplines, and the space to live as a counterculture to the craziness of this pressure-cooker life? It may well be that the advanced modern world requires more careful discernment than any previous age faced by Christians in history. But it is beyond question that the advanced modern world allows us less time to think about life and our own lives and offers us fewer tools to wrestle with its deepest challenges. Living with time in the advanced modern, globalized world is challenging as never before.

WHEN EVIL BECOMES COOL

Globalization compounds the difficulties and brings other challenges as we tackle such age-old problems as evil and suffering, and many of today's problems are now global in scale. For all the evidence of such horrors as Auschwitz and the Nazi death camps, we are certainly no more sinful and probably no more evil than previous generations of human beings. But we are more modern, and the modern global world both marginalizes traditional ways of viewing and handling evil and magnifies evil in crucial ways. For one thing, it has magnified destructiveness—not so much through the potency of our weapons as through the subtlety of such modern methods as the division of labor and the diffusion of responsibility.

Not so long ago, for instance, pornography in much of the world was the realm of the dirty old man, the shabby raincoat and the girly magazines in the seedy back streets shop, with deeper perversions lurking further back in the shadows. Today, with the global expansion of freedom through travel and technology, the global expansion of profit and the global expansion of crime, pornography is only a click of the button away from almost everyone, and a daily presence in the thoughts and lives of millions. And sex tourism, with its niche preferences for every conceivable taste and perversion, is there for all who wish to sign up.

Evil in the advanced modern world flaunts itself under the cover of the cool, the global, the connected and the accessible. It is now a matter of entitlement and a natural consumer option for millions. In both scale and style, modern evils such as sex trafficking, slavery and political corruption through influence peddling are global problems that are larger, harder and costlier to fight than ever before. Witness, for example, the feeble responses of Western corporate sponsors when rampant corruption is exposed in global sports such as soccer, cricket and the Olympics. Heaven forbid that integrity should trouble their bottom line! As even a few remarks show, this magnification of evil is profound, but at the same time it is merely one aspect of the many-sided, avalanche-like impact of globalization on our human lives and endeavors.

FROM A SINGULAR MODERNITY TO MULTIPLE MODERNITIES

The third grand transformation concerns the shift from what has been described as a "singular modernity" to "multiple modernities." The origins of the modern world can be traced in different ways, but it is common to describe a succession of world powers that were each the lead societies of the world in their time—Portugal with its intrepid navigators, Spain with its daring if rapacious explorers and colonizers, France with its military geniuses and its grand cultural creations, the Netherlands with its trading empire and its arts, Britain with its political innovations and its naval empire on which the sun never set, and the United States with its Pax Americana and its status as the global colossus of its time.

The effect of this was that whichever Western nation was the top dog in its day was automatically top dog in the world. Its privilege was to lead and shape modernity in its own image during its ascendancy, and its only rival was certain to come from among the other nations that made up the West, and that one after another were the world's lead societies in their turn. The rest of the world was always "the rest." It was different and it was behind, whether viewed as primitive, backward, reactionary, traditional, premodern, the majority world or developing. In a word, modernity was Western, so globalization was Westernization, Americanization and even Coca-Colonization. Fated always to be behind the West, it was the business of the rest to follow as best they could, though they could never hope to catch up.

Importantly, such arrogant conceit ran far deeper than obvious matters as economic and military power. It affected ideas too. The Enlightenment's secularization theory, for instance, was far more than an objective academic hypothesis reached by dispassionate minds in ivory towers. For it was self-serving. It held that as the world grew more modern, the world would steadily grow less religious, so that secularization was to be universal and inevitable. But the proponents of the theory could only hold this view because they projected the conditions of what was then the world's most modern continent, Europe, onto the whole world. "As Europe, so the world. Is that not obvious?" They therefore saw themselves in Europe as the global vanguard and ignored the special conditions that made Europe's secularity exceptional. (Plainly, the United States never did fit their theory. The United States took over from Europe and became the most modern country in the world while it was still the most religious of modern countries.)

More recently, a similar conceit surfaced in the United States in the preposterous claim that America's triumph in the Cold War meant that we were witnesses to "the end of history" itself and to its culmination in the permanent triumph of American-style liberal democracy. But this claim was Hegelian nonsense with an American twist, and it shared the same flaw and suffered the same fate as Europe's secularization theory. America's moment of global dominance was more fleeting than many people thought, but in its brief, dazzling light the theory absolutized the triumph of American liberal democracy and projected it onto history itself. The same nation that would not countenance the divine right of kings for a second fell for the equal hubris of absolutizing its own exceptionalism and announcing the end of all history other than its own. A "selfie moment" on a national scale if there ever was one.

In the case of both secularization and the end of history, the illusions have now been exposed. The world is still stubbornly religious, and what has ended is not history but the unquestioned dominance of liberal democracy. But more importantly, one of the most important consequences of globalization has been to extend modernity to more and more of the nations and to more and more of the earth in different ways. The result is that there are now many different expressions of modernity or multiple modernities. In other words, each nation has its own history and its own cultural values. It is therefore able to welcome modernity and adapt it to its own cultural situation at its own speed and in accord with its own principles and priorities. A phrase I have commonly heard in China on recent visits captures this perfectly: "It's our turn now." There are obvious limits to the autonomy each nation really has, for modernity has more of a say in shaping life than many realize. But theoretically every nation can adapt to modernity differently, and it is in this sense that we must recognize the fact of multiple modernities.

GLOBAL LORD, GLOBAL FOLLOWERS

What does this long overdue recognition mean for the church? As members of the world's most numerous faith and the world's first truly global religion, all we who are Christians must grapple responsibly with our own version of John Wesley's "I look on all the world as my parish," or René Dubos's maxim, "Think globally, act locally." The global world is no more ours to manage than it is ours to save. For that, we trust in a power far greater than ours, and a wisdom far higher than our own—the sovereignty and providence of God. Not for us the secular substitutes for providence, such as Thomas Hobbes's "leviathan" of the secular state or Adam Smith's "invisible hand" of the financial market. Not for us the deadly lure of global "giantism" that acts as if we are greater than we are, or the airy emptiness of pronouncing ourselves cosmopolitan "citizens of the world," without considering what that means. (Virginia Woolf: "As a woman I have no country. As a woman I want no country. As a woman my country is the whole world."[16])

But how can we be both global and local in ways that do justice to the magnificence of our Christian vision in the setting of today's intractable realities? With the incarnation of Jesus as our pattern, we glory on the one hand in sheer presence, and in bodily presence and therefore the primacy of the face to face—even under the pressure of our cell phones, smart devices and global communications. We gladly submit, too, to our Lord's wise call to the priority of dailiness. ("Give us this day our daily bread." "Each day has enough trouble of its own.") We are, after all, finite, and our little lives are fleeting—"as fast as a weaver's shuttle," as the psalmist expressed it. Here today, we are gone tomorrow, so all pretensions to human giantism are absurd and dangerous.

Among a thousand things, this means there will always be natural limits to the humanity and size of our churches. The optimum size of human communities that are bonded by face-to-face relationships, we are told, is around the magic number of 150 to 200. So as soon as any human community goes above that number, whether in the direction of a megachurch, with its tens of thousands, or a megacity, with its tens of millions, it requires coordinating in ways that are other than face to face and fully human—whether lightly through the interconnections of the social media or more heavy-handedly through authoritarian political control. The nature and impact of that form of coordination then become critical.

For better or worse, these different ways of bringing and holding people together have their own identifiable dynamics that in the end will always determine the quality of the larger community. Modern megacities have reached a size that creates intrinsic problems of their own, and there can be grandiose hi-tech forms of the church that have similar problems. They will appeal to the techno-gnostics who lionize the brilliance of disembodied video images and abstractions and disparage what St. Francis humbly called "Brother Ass." But they will never prove to be the wave of the future. The neighborhood parish church is not just the church of the past but the church of the future. Scorned and overshadowed though it may be at times, it will never be outmoded while humans are human and have bodies.

But that said, there is another side of the challenge too. "For God so loved the world" (Jn 3:16), and we must too. After all, we can now see "everything in the world as it happens," and we can now reach "almost anywhere and everywhere in twenty-four hours" through our travel and communications. So we must raise our game too, "lengthening our cords and strengthening our stakes" so that our hi-tech tents are more capacious and welcoming than ever. We must do "our utmost for His highest" to the fullest extent in all the spheres of our daily callings, knowing that as we do this together, the hands and hearts and love of the Christian community can stretch around the world more extensively and more effectively than those of any other faith on earth.

Probably no single local church in history has done this more daringly, generously and effectively than Pastor Rick Warren's Saddleback

Church in Southern California, but there are others too. At the same time, our prayers must reach out more widely and more urgently on behalf of governments and all that makes our world stable and just and free. Only so can we be worthy of our Lord's love for the world as a whole. And only so can our passion for justice and our generosity and compassion keep crossing new boundaries to help people who are decidedly not like us and who would never have been neighbors before the age of television and travel. Only so can we defy the people-like-us limits of much human concern and remain true to Jesus' story of the good Samaritan on a higher and wider level than ever before.

Is such a balance between the global and the local possible and sustainable? Will the global church achieve it and rise to the challenge of the hour and be a vital player in the future of humanity? Will we wage spiritual warfare on behalf of global powers? These are no easy tasks, yet the implications of multiple modernities go directly to such momentous issues, as we shall see. Indeed, each of these three grand transformations is momentous, as are the issues they raise, and to explore them would take us far beyond our present concerns. Yet at the very least, our global vision must take in the widest horizons of the fascinating, turbulent and volatile world of our day. This is the world of our time, and this is our moment before the Lord. Only by recognizing it can we hope to shoulder the responsibility of serving God's purposes at such a time and in such a generation.

⇒ A Prayer ⇐

O LORD OUR GOD, before you the cosmos itself is smaller than a speck of dust, and beside you our boldest dreams and highest goals are puny. Stretch the horizons of our hearts and minds with the immensity of your glory, the depths of your truth, the boundlessness of your love and the wonder of your grace, so that our trust in you may be as unshakable as the heavens, and our compassion for our neighbors across the world may be as deep as the oceans and as wide as their global needs. So may we be your people, with your heart, your hands and your love for your world. Through Jesus Christ our Lord, Amen.

QUESTIONS FOR DISCUSSION

1. Where do we see examples of the Babel-like drive to become "as God" today? What are the arguments and attitudes that make it so natural and so hard to argue against?

2. Where does the tension between the *global* and the *local* and *daily* hit you and your family? How have you tried to cope in balancing the impossible demands? Where do you *think globally* in good ways?

3. It is easy to react against such past wrongs as imperialism and colonialism, but what is a better way forward that prays for and cares for the whole world while avoiding the pitfalls for the past?

chapter two

The Greatest Challenge Ever

I n 1989 I was privileged to be invited to address a plenary session of the second Lausanne Congress in Manila on the subject of "Mission and Modernity." It was challenging because I was allotted only seventeen minutes to explore a topic that was not only vast but unfamiliar to most people engaged in mission. I did my best within the limits, and after the session was over I went out into the foyer where a missionary approached me.

"I didn't hear all that you said," she told me, "and I didn't understand all that I heard. But allow me to ask you one question. Why on earth did they ask a man to speak on maternity?"

Modernity mistaken for maternity? The one term is novel to many people and the other is familiar, but the way we use the familiar term can throw light on the less familiar. If maternity is a single word that covers all the broad constellation of things that make up motherhood, modernity is equally simple and comprehensive. It covers all the dazzling range of ideas and institutions that make up our modern world—not just ideas but cities, airplanes, nuclear power stations, businesses and offices, cars, televisions, computers and smartphones. In short, modernity is far more than a matter of ideas.

To be sure, the terms *modernism* and *postmodernism* (each ending in *-ism*) are sets of ideas, but *modernity* (ending in *-ity*) refers to far more than ideas. It certainly includes distinctive modern ideas—for example, relativism, skepticism, efficiency and calculability—but it includes far more, so that it is a mistake to confuse *postmodernism* with *postmodernity*. Several implications stem from this distinction, not least that someone who is modernist or postmodernist in their thinking can change their minds and abandon their outworn ideas in a second. Modernity, however, being far more than a set of ideas, is not so easily dispensed with, even if someone comes to actively dislike or oppose it. Indeed, it is inconceivable to think of a true postmodernity, in the sense of a world after modernity, short of an unimaginable global disaster.

Why on earth do such distinctions matter? Far more than a matter of semantics, they are crucial to the way Christians in the West size up the challenges we are facing today. If anyone were to tell most congregations in the West that the modern church is facing the greatest challenge the church has ever encountered, chances are that he or she would be met with puzzled looks. Like an undiagnosed cancer, the nature and source of the danger we face is not on the minds of most Western Christians, so they would respond blankly. Certainly, they would appreciate what it is to face scathing attacks from prominent atheists, they would see the ravages of radical Islam in other countries, and they would certainly know of the steadily mounting, uncalled-for animosity from certain sectors of the press and the cultural elites, but the greatest challenge ever? Greater even than, say, persecution or heresy? That would surely be considered exaggerated and alarmist, even in an age when it is routine for modern communications to grab people by the scruff of the neck to commandeer attention to their cause.

It is modernity in this fuller, wider sense, not just modernism, that represents the greatest challenge the church has ever faced. But why? Because modernity has done more damage to the church than all the persecutors of the church and all the heretics combined. From Nero and Diocletian to Stalin, Mao Zedong and the ayatollahs and imams, the attacks of the persecutors have been frontal and the assaults of the heretics have been central and insidious, but to this point they have not done half the damage caused by modernity. Indeed, the blood of the martyrs has been the seed of the church, and the assaults of the heretics have served to sharpen the faith and trigger the creation of such classic statements of historic orthodoxy as the Apostles' Creed and the Nicene Creed. Yet so far there has been no similar heroic response from the modern church rising to overcome the challenges of the advanced modern world.

Let me be clear. If modernity is a deadly challenge to the church, it is not a frontal challenge in the way that hostile ideologies are. The new atheists, for example, are like the communists earlier. They are implacably opposed to the Christian faith and make no bones about their opposition to the Christian faith and their exclusion of Christians. (In the much-quoted words of the Harvard geneticist Richard Lewontin, "We cannot allow a Divine foot in the door.")[1] "No faith wanted here," they say in effect, separating out people of faith as Nazi guards did certain Jews on their arrival at Auschwitz-Birkenau.

That crude, open kind of opposition is certainly the sort of challenge posed by certain modernists such as the new atheists, but it is not the challenge of modernity. After all, there is a vital difference between *secularism* (as a *personal philosophy*), *separationism* (as a legal and *political policy* advocating the strict separation of religion and public life) and *secularization* (as a *process* that is part and parcel of modernization). The three terms are commonly confused, and while they overlap in having the same end result, they are entirely different ways to getting there, and the differences are crucial. The first is a philosophy, the second is a political policy and the third is a process. Modernism as a philosophy may oppose faith outright, but modernity does not. Its damage is not through opposition but through seduction and distortion. It doesn't say, for example, "No faith allowed here" but "No faith is needed here." Contrary to Jesus and the Torah, modernity claims that man can now live "by bread alone," or rather by science, technology, management and marketing alone. Secularists do not want God, whereas the secularized have no need of God, and that is only one of the many seductions and distortions of modernity.

We saw earlier that the long-dominant secularization theory was a false and biased account of the impact of modernity on religion. The world has steadily become more modern and religion has not disappeared as proponents of the theory predicted. Indeed, in many ways the world is as furiously religious as ever. But it would be equally wrong to stop there and argue that because religion appears to be flourishing in the modern world, it is unchanged. Religion has not disappeared, as its critics once thought and hoped, but neither has it remained unchanged. Modernity has shaped religions in distinctive ways that for some are inconsequential and for others highly critical. In short, if we are to be faithful to our Lord and be "in the world" but "not of the world," we have to understand the world.

This is not the place for a full account of the impact of modernity on the Christian faith and the Christian church. That ground has been well covered. Instead, let me merely open up three examples of the sort of damage modernity is inflicting on the Christian faith and the church. In each case, the trends behind the damage would not matter to many other faiths, but they are critical and damaging to Christian faith because of the nature of the gospel and the character of Christian truth. Once again, my concern is not historical or analytical, but the significance for discipleship. Christians are called to be in the world but not of it, so modernity is simply the world in a modern form that is surely the most powerful, pervasive and pressurizing ever. And therein lies the challenge posed to the church. Either the Christian church must prevail over these modern seductions and distortions of the world of modernity, or the church must succumb to an abject worldliness and be exposed for both its cultural weakness and its failure to be faithful to its Lord.

PICKING AND CHOOSING

A first and crucially important distortion comes from the way the modern world shifts us from a stance under authority to one of preference—or expressed more carefully, tends to undermine all forms of authority other than its own and replaces them with the sense that all responses are merely a matter of preference. It goes without saying that authority is central and crucial to both the Jewish and Christian faiths. Rabbi Jonathan Sacks points out that Leviticus is perhaps "the key text of Judaism," and tradition came to call it by its first word *Vayikra*, which means "He called."[2] The three terms "He said," "He spoke" and "He commanded" preface many of the instructions in the book, and together they speak of God's undisputed authority, though they also carry a note of endearment and love. Unique among the gods believed in throughout history, the Lord is transcendent, so what he says is truth, binding truth, because it addresses us as authority. To dilute this authority is to dismiss the Lord himself.

For Christians, "Jesus is Lord" is the central conviction and confession of the Christian faith. In the words of the previously skeptical but then believing Thomas, we are followers of Jesus because we have reached the warranted conviction: "My Lord and my God" (Jn 20:28). Christians believe that Jesus Christ is fully God become fully human, the unique, sure and sufficient revelation of the very being, character and purposes of the transcendent God, beside whom there is no other god, and beside whom there is no other name by which we must be saved.

The follower of Jesus is therefore a person under authority, living before the transcendent majesty of God and unashamed to be so. What God tells us, we trust. And what God tells us to do, we obey. We therefore gladly acknowledge that we are not self-created, we are not self-sufficient, and we are not autonomous. No one in the world has a higher view and more solid notion of freedom than Jews and Christians. The Book of Common Prayer addresses God "whose service is perfect freedom." But this freedom has a threefold framework, so it is never viewed as autonomous. First, it is understood as a gift from God and not an achievement of our own. Second, it is always relational, and therefore it is experienced and it matures only in relationship with our Master, our brothers and sisters, and our fellow citizens. And third, it is always lived out within the framework of the teaching of Jesus and the Scriptures. Jewish and Christian freedom is freedom within the form of the truth of God's way of life.

This means that Christian faith is a faith constituted by the authority of Jesus. Whatever Jesus himself commands, or whatever other authority is given, Jesus' stamp of authority is the final word for Christians who would follow Jesus faithfully. Jesus' own teaching and his attitude toward the total truthfulness and supreme authority of the Bible, God's inspired Word, make the Scriptures our final rule and authority. What the Scriptures say, God says, and what God says, we obey.

Critics dismiss this view of authority as quaint and rigid in the world of modernity. And modernity tends to render it unthinkable in a thousand ways, subtly but systematically. For a start, there is the inescapable presence and power of *pluralization*—the process by which the proliferation of endless choice and incessant change increases at all levels of modern life. If "everyone is now everywhere," then everyone is aware of "all those others" all the time, and with all the awareness of others comes the reminder of all the choices and changes that are open to us too at any moment. And if there is a wide array of choice today, tomorrow will bring even more.

To be sure, the dizzying array of choices is most obvious in a supermarket or a shopping mall, but the allure of choice has spread far beyond the walls of official consumerland. From breakfast cereals to restaurants and cuisines to sexual identities and temptations to possible sexual arrangements of all types to self-help techniques and philosophies of life, we are offered an infinite array of choices, and the focus is always on choice as *choosing* rather than choice as the *content* of what is chosen. Just choose. Simply choose. Experiment. Try it out for yourself. How else will you know unless you have tried it? After all, there are always others, there is always someone or something more, so unless you try them how are you to know whether you have missed the possible holiday, relationship or philosophy that might really hit the jackpot?

"Love to one is only a barbarity," Nietzsche wrote in *Beyond Good and Evil*, "for it is exercised at the expense of all others. Love to God also."[3]

There you have it. Even God is reduced to consumer choice, and when truth is taken out of the equation, sticking to one choice is no longer a matter of intellectual conviction but a sign of timidity as well as folly. Surely, the unspoken adspeak tells us, you should always be open-minded, for the genuine freethinker will always wish to choose and keep choosing, to experiment and keep on experimenting. Our freedom is the freedom to choose, regardless of whether our choice is right or wrong, wise or stupid. So long as we can choose, we are free. Choosing is all that matters. Truth, goodness and authority are irrelevant to the central act and the main event: you are the sovereign chooser, and you are free to exercise your sovereign right to choose and choose and choose again in whatever way you like—until all choices seem the same and each one shrivels into insignificance.

Anyone thinking along can immediately see why freedom of conscience and conscientious objection are routinely dismissed today. Freedom of choice and freedom of conscience are entirely different. Freedom of choice has become autonomous and a matter of entitlement, whereas freedom of conscience was never free. It was a duty and therefore duty bound and not free. Conscience was once respected precisely because a person was duty bound, or bound by the dictates of conscience—"Here I stand. I can do no other." But in today's world, freedom of conscience is confused with freedom of choice and therefore rendered dutiless and shorn of its rights.

The net effect of this concentration on choosing lies at the heart of our modern consumer society. Choice at the expense of the content of the choice elevates the sovereign chooser and devalues the content of the choice and reduces it to a preference. Does it matter whether you choose Wheaties, Bircher Muesli or Irish oatmeal as your breakfast, or football, baseball or golf as your sport? But then, does it matter whether you worship on Friday with the Muslims, Saturday with the Jews, Sunday with the Christians or not at all? Or whether your sister-in-law is straight or lesbian, or your boss is a heterosexual womanizer, a homosexual or was once a woman? There are different strokes for different folks. We are all different and all our lifestyles and journeys are different, so who are we to judge when we haven't walked in another person's moccasins? This is my choice. That is yours. We are all free to choose differently, and our choices only amount to different preferences, so who is to say who is right? Or to care what anyone else chooses? And what business do any of us have to judge other people's preferences?

Whatever.

When such autonomous, free-choice consumerism washes over society from the shopping mall to the bedroom, the office and the ballot box, the result is predictable. What will be the price of obedience to authority, and what will be the respect accorded to principled dissent? Choice—unbounded autonomous, subjective sovereign individual choice—is the playboy king of consumerland, and with comfort and convenience as his closest courtiers and cronies, he now rules much of life. Authority and obedience are therefore banished together. They are the unwelcome spoilsports whose entry might ruin the fantasy game of infinite choices. The result is no surprise—a grave crisis of authority within the church, and a rash of positions and interpretations that in any clearer thinking generation would be frankly seen as the rejection of the authority of Jesus and the Scriptures that they are.

Evangelicals are especially vulnerable to this distortion of choice because of the exaggerated place they give to choice in the call to conversion. It may even be their Achilles' heel. Whereas the Jews are the *chosen people*, so that their faith is their destiny, Evangelicals are a *choosing people*, and their faith is often merely their decision. The step of faith is of course a choice, the most important and fully responsible choice a person ever makes. But when the overwhelming emphasis is put on choice as an act of decision, choosing becomes everything, but it can then suffer the fate of many modern choices and shrink to being lightweight, changeable and nonbinding. Choice and change are close companions, and those who decide for a faith because they choose to believe it can as easily defect from the faith when they choose not to.

Contrast this modern casualness with the early church's deep theology surrounding conversion and especially the costly stress on the public witness of the sacrament of baptism. This was a direct and deliberate counterpoint to the Roman practice of sacrament. For the Romans, the *sacramentum* was far more serious than a normal oath in a law court. It was the solemn vow by which a person gave his or her word before an authority and put his or her life in forfeit as a guarantee of what had been sworn. Those who had given their *sacramentum* were then *sacer*. They were "given to the gods" if they violated the vow. They had given their sacred bond and they were no longer their own. For example, the *sacramentum* was the oath of allegiance sworn by Roman soldiers to the emperor as they joined the legions and by gladiators as they went out to fight and die.

For Christians, then, baptism was no casual choice. It was a public vow, a decisive break with the past and a solemn binding oath of allegiance to Jesus, sworn to God and before God—and before their fellow believers and the watching world. This was probably one reason why there were so many deathbed baptisms, such as the Emperor Constantine's ("I am now numbered among the people of God. . . . I shall now set out for myself rules of life which befit God").[4] People did not wish to die unforgiven, but neither did they wish to commit themselves any earlier than they needed to live under a vow (*sacramentum*) that was so costly and so binding. Choice today can always be casual, whereas the covenantal vow of faith is costly because we commit ourselves to Jesus and mortgage our very selves as we do so. We have chosen, and we are committed. We have picked up our crosses, and there is no turning back. We are no longer our own.

The modern temptation to trivialize choice is not new. It ultimately stems from our human fallenness as truth seekers who are always inevitably truth twisters too. Instead of seeking to shape our desires according to the reality of God's truth, we seek to shape reality according to our desires—and modern consumerism aids and abets us as never before. St. Augustine addressed the problem in the fifth century, and his protest against the Manichaean distortions of the Scriptures could apply equally to those who attempt to rationalize their justification of homosexual marriage: "For you people who believe in the gospel what you choose to believe, and do not believe what you choose not to believe, believe yourselves rather than the gospel."[5]

Just so today, Christian advocates of homosexual and lesbian revisionism believe in themselves and in the sexual revolution rather than the gospel. They therefore twist the Scriptures to make reality fit their desires rather than making their desires fit the truths of the Scriptures. In Søren Kierkegaard's stinging term, they are "kissing Judases" who betray Jesus with an interpretation.

Protestant liberalism has long sauntered down this road, brazenly repudiating the authority of Jesus for the successive authorities of the Enlightenment and post-Enlightenment worldviews. To paraphrase George Canning's description of those who were fellow travelers of the revolutionary Jacobins, liberal revisionists are "friends of every faith except their own." In the process whole churches and entire denominations have effectively chased a mirage and committed spiritual and institutional suicide and rendered themselves as irrelevant as they are unfaithful.

The tragic story of extreme Protestant revisionism makes it all the harder to witness the pitiful attempts of Evangelical revisionists to follow the Gadarene rush over the cliff. As I write, for example, the pastor of an Evangelical church in San Francisco has announced that he regards the way of Jesus as "destructive" to human flourishing as it is now understood. He therefore proposes that it should be relaxed to allow for the more "compassionate" and contemporary lifestyle of homosexual marriage. Sadly for him and his followers, he does not understand the lessons of the Bible and history—that he is courting spiritual and institutional suicide for himself and for those he is leading astray. Though to be fair, he and others like him are only reaping what others sowed with such fanfare a generation ago. For were we not solemnly sold a barrel of nonsense in the form of maxims that all good seeker-sensitive and audience-driven churches were to pursue? Here is one example from a well-known Christian marketing consultant: "It is also critical that we keep in mind a fundamental principle of Christian communication: the audience, not the message, is sovereign."

The audience is sovereign? No! Let it be repeated a thousand times, *no*! When reaching out as the church of Jesus, the message of the gospel and Jesus the Lord of the message is alone sovereign— and never, never, never the audience, however needy, however attractive, however prestigious or well-heeled an audience may be. Yes, like the apostle Paul we are to be Jews to the Jews, Gentiles to the Gentiles, and all things to all our fellow humans, excluding no one in any age or any sphere or condition of life. That, of course, is one side of the truth of the seeker-sensitive approach. But the other side of the truth is that we are always and only to be all things to all people, not in order to join them but rather, like Paul, to bring them back to Jesus.

All such Evangelicals should search their hearts. For a generation now the air has been thick with talk of "changing the world," but who is changing whom? There is no question that the world would like to change the church. In area after area only the church stands between the world and its success over issues such as sexuality. Unquestionably the world would like to change the church, but does the church still want to change the world, or is its only concern to change the church in the light of the world? Something is rotten in the state of Evangelicalism, and all too often it is impossible to tell who is changing whom.

There are always essential questions to ask of anyone we hear or anything we read. What is being said? Is it true? And what of it? All three questions are discounted in our modern age of information, but as Christians we must never allow the truth question to be removed from its central place. To be sure, faithfulness is costly in the short term. It is upstream and against the flow, and the flow that was once politically correct can suddenly become a raging and life-threatening intolerance. But costly though that stand may be, it is never as costly as the long-term price of rejecting the authority of Jesus and abandoning the way of life in the gospel. Our Lord warned of that very danger: "Do not fear those who kill the body but are unable to kill the soul; but rather fear Him who is able to destroy both soul and body in hell" (Mt 10:28).

Today's Evangelical revisionists should take sober note. Time and again I tremble when I hear or read their flimsy arguments. They may be lionized by the wider advocates of the sexual revolution for fifteen minutes, because they are siding with that wider culture in undermining the clear teaching of Jesus and the Bible that stands in their way. For there is no question that Jesus, the Scriptures and Christian tradition all stand resolutely in their way. But in truth, the sexual revolution has no real interest in such Evangelicals, and they will be left as roadkill as the revolution blitzkrieg gathers speed. But that is nothing compared with the real tragedy of the revisionists. It is no light thing for anyone to set themselves above and against the authority of Jesus and his Scriptures. The apostle Peter betrayed Jesus and was restored, but Judas stands as the warning for all who betray Jesus for their personal, sexual or political interests and condemn themselves for their disloyalty.

Both Jesus and the apostle Peter tell us to "remember Lot's wife" (Lk 17:33), but our Christian revisionists should remember Lot himself. Having chosen the benefits and privileges of living in the well-watered garden country of Sodom, having married into their social circles and having worked his way up into the inner leadership of the city, Lot was suddenly confronted by his moment of truth. He had been utterly naive and deluded in trusting the Sodomites. When the chips were down, they had no respect for his hospitality, no time for his different moral standards, and they threatened to deal with him as brutally as with his guests: "This one came in as an alien, and already he is acting like a judge; now we will treat you worse than them" (Gen 19:9).

Poor Lot had become a joke even to his in-laws. In spite of all his efforts and contrary to all that he imagined, he had still not arrived, and he was never accepted as he imagined. He was always the alien—as Abraham never forgot that he was and was respected for being. We of course should always be resident aliens as faithful Christians who are in the world but not of it—regardless of the world's pressure on us to change with the times and line up with them on the so-called right side of history.

PRIVATELY ENGAGING, PUBLICLY IRRELEVANT

The second example of the distortions of modernity is the tendency of the modern world to shift religion from a position of integration to one of fragmentation. A central and unmistakable characteristic of all three Abrahamic faiths is their uncompromising demand for integrity and integration. For Jews this integration of faith and life is to be under the Torah. For Christians it is to be under the lordship of Jesus. And for Muslims it is to be under the Qur'an or sharia. Many other religions would never make such a demand—for devotees of the New Age movement, for instance, what they do when they meditate has little or nothing to say about how they read a spreadsheet or run a board meeting. But for followers of Jesus, integration is a nonnegotiable demand. If God is Lord of heaven and earth and all there is, his lordship must cover everything or mean nothing. His writ and his rule of life must run everywhere.

So Christian lives must be true all the way through, and every Christian must be true everywhere and in everything. "Not a hoof shall be left behind," Moses tells the Pharaoh bluntly when the Egyptians wish to compromise over letting some of God's people go and only go some way (Ex 10:26). "Why do you call Me, 'Lord, Lord,'" Jesus said to his disciples, "and do not do what I say?" (Lk 6:46). Or in the simple but radical words of John R. Mott, "If Jesus Christ is not Lord of all, he is not Lord at all."

It is easy to speak, write or sing about the lordship of Jesus with heartfelt sincerity, but that very passion can mask the fact that it is harder than ever to live it out in the advanced modern world. In the traditional world an integrated life hardly needed thought at all, as our ancestors mostly lived in small villages and mid-sized towns, where community was organic and face to face; it was relatively easy for most people to walk or ride around the whole community in a short time, and faith went everywhere naturally—especially when it was the only faith in town. But that world has gone. At the heart of modernity are the two processes of *pluralization* and *differentiation*, the former being the throwing up of endless others, choices and alternatives, and the latter being the throwing up of all sorts of complex and different spheres in life as cities explode, travel reaches further and further, and communications are faster and more inclusive all the time.

Take a sprawling, modern, freeway metropolitan area such as Los Angeles (or Shanghai or Mexico City). Many people think nothing of driving seventy-five to one hundred miles to go to church on Sunday and an equal distance to go to work on Monday morning. Then add in the places where they shop or go to the cinema, and all the places they may take their children to, from schools to sports to amusement parks and beaches. The result is a vast network of places, linked together only by cars and endless driving, with each place having its own different purpose, priorities and ways of life—in a word, a world of fragmentation.

Needless to say, the LA way of life is merely one of physical or geographical fragmentation, but the same *differentiation* (a fancy word for "splitting apart" and sometimes "smashing to smithereens") is happening in many other areas of life too. Thanks to the pill and the libertine freedom of the wider sexual revolution, the modern world has differentiated between sex and love and split apart love and commitment, marriage and having children, and having children and taking care of them ourselves. All these once-integrated areas and ideas are now different matters of individual freedom and choice.

This means that lives integrated throughout by faith are harder to live and rarer to find than ever, so if there is to be integration, it will now be difficult and will have to be self-conscious and deliberate. For, the obvious tendency, or temptation, in a fragmented world is to go with the flow and to accept all the different places and the separate issues in life as natural, and then to live slightly differently in each place or treat the separate issues separately without realizing it. That fragmentation can of course be aggravated in turn by deficient theologies, such as a warm-hearted but empty-headed pietism. It was precisely such an unconsciously fragmented faith that prompted the damning comment on the Californian churches by a local historian. The Christian faith in California, he said, was "privately engaging, publicly irrelevant." It was fragmented, not integrated. The lordship of Christ over life had been scattered into countless bits—death by a thousand fragmentations. Worse still, as a Jewish witticism has long recognized, for believers to keep a low profile can be a mark of cowardice: *Incognito ergo sum*—"I am invisible. Therefore I am."

A WORLD WITHOUT WINDOWS

A third critical distortion effected by modernity is the general shift in consciousness from the supernatural to the secular. It would be absurd to think that premodern people were always piously praying or were really fundamentally different from us in living with their heads in the supernatural clouds. They too had to cook their dinner and dispose of their trash. But among many profound differences between their world and ours, one was that for them *the unseen was not unreal*. They lived in the same seven to eleven waking world as we do, but their everyday seen world, and their daily mundane activities such as business, farming and sex, were understood in light of the unseen world. The seen was only part of the world, and the unseen was in fact the more real. Whereas for us the unseen is generally unreal and largely irrelevant.

Rabbi Jonathan Sacks points out that the rationalist and the mystic stand at the two poles. "For the mystic, the invisible is real, the visible unreal, a mere mask hiding the Divine. The rationalist sees the universe and wonders whether God really exists. The mystic sees God and wonders whether the universe really exists."[6] Plainly, the advanced modern world is closer to the rationalist pole. We may not understand such mysteries as quarks, black holes and anti-matter, but our real world mostly includes things we can see, hear, touch, smell, weigh, measure and calculate. For the modern realist the real world is the world we engage from Monday to Friday, especially the world of work, and not Saturday and Sunday. We live, as Peter Berger puts it, in a "world without windows."[7]

There is considerable irony to this cave-bound captivity, for there are many unseen things that we have no problem believing— the past and the future, for example. Science itself delves far beyond the reach of our five senses when it explores the world of subatomic quarks and pentaquarks. And even secular anthropologists tell us that the ability to experience and talk about things beyond our everyday world of the five senses is the key to the rise of Homo sapiens and the cognitive revolution. It sets us apart, they say, from other species of animals and gives rise to both religion and art. As Yuval Harari notes, "As far as we know, only Sapiens can talk about entire kinds of entities that they have never seen, touched, or smelled."[8]

Yet regardless of such considerations, the thought police of our day permit only a view of reality like that of the cave dwellers in Plato's famous parable of the cave. The world bathed in the sunshine outside is off-limits and strictly dismissed as fiction. In G. K. Chesterton's less pejorative picture, our modern view of reality is like that of a slightly drowsy middle-aged man right after a good lunch.

David Ben-Gurion, the primary founder and first prime minister of Israel, once quipped that "In Israel, in order to be a realist, you must believe in miracles." We have almost precisely reversed that statement, for advanced modernity tends to make people lose an entire dimension of reality in the name of realism. It reinforces the naturalistic worldview of scientism and the secularist and renders meaningless the supernatural worldview of the Christian. But in this case the problem of our spiritual myopia long predates the rise of the modern world. The advanced modern world only puts the capstone on the problem. Both the Old and New Testaments are alive with a vibrant awareness of the supernatural as a vital part of God's created order, and the opening words of the Nicene Creed express the biblical worldview well: "We believe in one God, the Father, the Almighty, maker of heaven and earth, *of all that is, seen and unseen*" (emphasis added). After all, the apostle Paul reminds the Colossians in the Lycus River Valley, Jesus himself is the very image of "the invisible God," and he created all things "visible and invisible" (Col 1:15-16).

In this biblical view of the world and reality, the seen and the unseen are both real, and the believer can count on both in living the life of faith in the full reality of God's created order. Much of the Old Testament would be meaningless and unintelligible if this account of reality is removed. "O LORD, I pray, open his eyes that he may see," Elisha asked God when his servant was panicking at the sight of the enemy armies surrounding his city. "And the LORD opened the servant's eyes and he saw; and behold, the mountain was full of horses and chariots of fire all around Elisha" (2 Kings 6:16-17).

The same is even more evident in the New Testament. Jesus of Nazareth burst on the scene in Galilee filled and armed with the power of the Spirit of God. Apart from the Spirit, Jesus was only the carpenter's son, and everyone knew his father and his family. But the Spirit and all he did in the power of the Spirit were his credentials that made him more than "the son of Joseph." "THE SPIRIT OF THE LORD IS UPON ME," he declares in his liberating Jubilee manifesto of the kingdom of God, as he announces his grand work to rescue, restore and renew humanity (Lk 4:18-21). And Jesus not only said; he did it. He displayed that power on our behalf and demonstrated that he was indeed the Christ, the long-promised Messiah, the anointed One, by preaching and teaching in the power of the Spirit, by healing people like us from all kinds of sickness, by delivering people like us who were bound by demons and evil spirits, and by directly discerning the hearts and motives of all the humans he encounters. And again and again, Jesus did these things *before* he explained them, or in doing them he challenged people to figure out what these actions were saying about who he was. The kingdom of God was demonstrated as much as it was declared, or rather the reality of the kingdom was declared in the demonstration.

But that is the moment when we, his followers, came in, for it was apt that the followers of Jesus were called Christians by their neighbors in Antioch. Jesus the Christ was God's anointed One, but he did not hold his anointing and his power to himself. His followers were to be the "little Christs," the little anointed and empowered ones. All four Gospels recount the same prophecy of John the Baptist that a central work of the Messiah would be to baptize or to immerse his followers with the Holy Spirit as he had been, and Luke adds, "and [with] fire" (Lk 3:16). For as his work expanded, Jesus gave the same Spirit and the same anointing to empower the chosen Twelve and then the Seventy, telling them to proclaim that "the kingdom of heaven is at hand," and as they go, "Heal *the* sick, raise *the* dead, cleanse *the* lepers, cast out demons" (Mt 10:7-8).

Then, on the Day of Pentecost Jesus gave that same titanic gift to the whole church, commissioning them for their task on behalf of the whole of humanity and promising his now intrepid band of followers that through the gift of his Spirit they would do even greater deeds than he had done when he was with them. No wonder the story that exploded from this commission was called the Acts of the Apostles rather than the Message of the Apostles. The first Christians spoke in stunning power and acted in equally stunning power. The gospel, Paul reminded the church in Corinth, had arrived not with mere words, "but in demonstration of the Spirit and of power" (1 Cor 2:4). But it was not just their message that was to be marked with power, it was their very lives, for how, apart from the Spirit, were they to be able to overcome and live the revolutionary new way of Jesus?

Put all the self-help philosophies, techniques and seminars together, bring in all the counselors, psychologists and psychiatrists ever trained, and never in a million years would humanity as it was, and is, ever be capable of achieving a new humanity. Nietzsche saw this centuries later and said it all in a book title. We humans are *Human, All Too Human*. In *Thus Spoke Zarathustra*, he described the human being as "a rope stretched between animal and the Superman."[9] Just as we look down on the antics of monkeys and laugh at their inferiority to us, so he claimed that the superhuman would one day look down and laugh at our human antics. For if we are all too human as we are, man has to overcome man, he argued, and the great overcomer that he proclaimed at the heart of his counter-gospel was to be the self-made "Superman" (the übermensch or overman).

For Christians, such a view is no less utopian than the self-help guru and far more dangerous, for there has never been such a superman, and the very attempt to become one has produced only dangerous egomaniacs and dictators. Human beings can never overcome themselves by themselves. The only possible "overcomers" are fallen and fallible human beings who have been rescued ("saved"), who then turn their lives over to Jesus and are immersed and filled with the power of his Spirit, and thus they can do by the Spirit what they could never do by themselves. Thus the "saint" is not a superhuman who has overcome, won a halo and is now qualified to be prayed to at a shrine, but the same old sinner as the rest of us—penitent, forgiven and filled with the Spirit of God.

The point is inescapable. For the early Christians the supernatural as directly divine power was entirely natural, and the unseen was gloriously real as a crucial dimension of Christians living as the vanguard of restored humanity. The many signs and wonders performed were not a little bonus thrown in for the credulous masses of the prescientific age but a glimpse into the divine energy of the kingdom of God that Jesus had unleashed into the broken world in power. Through the power of the Spirit of Jesus, the kingdom of heaven was now present and active, working to rescue and restore humanity. As in heaven, so on earth, Jesus taught us to pray, and it was the presence and power of the Spirit that made that union of heaven and earth possible.

In the power of the Holy Spirit, the power of sin and the power of the evil one had met their match. Without it the story of the church would have been as brief and insignificant as that of thousands of other tiny religious sects in the rainbow diversity of the Roman world. But with the power of the Spirit the church could live the life of the kingdom of God and then, like the mountainous stone in the vision of Daniel, it could fill the earth and outlast the passing parade of world empires and superpowers—*but always, only, and so long as it was by the power of the Spirit of God.* Jesus, the Son of God, is the Father's greatest gift to humanity, and the Spirit of Jesus is the greatest gift of Jesus to his followers and the essential requirement for living his way of life and fulfilling his Great Commission.

That presence of the Spirit and the same power in the unseen world continued unabated down the centuries in many parts of the widening Christian world. There are clear references to the close connection between of baptism with water and baptism with the Spirit and to the persistence of ordinary believers involved in supernatural healing and deliverance. In Alexandria, for instance, Origen (c. AD 184–254) commented that Christians cast out demons "merely by prayer and the simplest commands that the plainest person can use, because, for the most part, it is unlettered persons who perform this work."[10] This work is not for the great ones alone. Armed with the Spirit, he says, anyone can do it.

This supernatural ministry continued at least as far as the fifth century and the time of St. Augustine, who started almost as a cessationist, teaching that Christians should no longer expect the continuation of miracles. He changed his mind, however, under the sheer weight of the facts, and later in his life he wrote, "I realized how many miracles were occurring in our own day and which were so like the miracles of old and also how wrong it would be to allow the memory of these marvels of divine power to perish from among our people."[11] In his hometown of Hippo alone he knew witnesses of more than seventy attested miracles. There was no Billy Graham and no C. S. Lewis in the early church. Nor could there be, and such signs and wonders were one of the main ways the gospel spread in the Roman empire.

From then onward, however, the church achieved its own power and glory, and as faith grew fashionable, the increase in secular power meant a corresponding decrease in spiritual power. Slowly the next centuries showed discernible trends that steadily reduced the earlier reliance on the power of the Spirit, so that as we move closer to our own day it becomes clear that in much of the church the unseen is no more real for Christians than it is for atheists, and many otherwise orthodox Christians are in effect operational

atheists or atheists unawares. To be sure, Christians still affirm the
historic creeds, and we say we believe in the Holy Spirit and in
prayer and the supernatural, but for many they are now only words.
Prayer for many Christians is mostly a matter of what is prayed in
public worship, healings and deliverances are comparatively rare,
direct spiritual discernment is infrequent—at least in comparison
with the Gospels and the book of Acts—and for many the Holy
Spirit is the forgotten member of the divine Trinity.

A TRIO OF TRENDS

Somewhat simplified, three separate trends, sometimes singly and
sometimes overlapping, have done the major damage down the
centuries to the church's experience of the living power of the Holy
Spirit and its recognition of the realities of the unseen world.

First, there has often been a tendency toward a false and unbib-
lical specialization, so that spiritual power came to be seen as
limited to certain people, rather than all Christians, and to certain
places, rather than anywhere God's people are present. "They," the
saints as special people, are obviously the gifted and anointed ones,
and "we," the rest of us who are not so gifted and anointed, can then
delegate our responsibility to them, with relief. In the long Catholic
centuries, for example, the supernatural power of all believers was
curtailed in the same way as the priesthood of all believers and the
calling of all believers. It became limited to certain special holy men
and women and above all to certain saints, for whom miracles
became an attested part of their canonization. And it was limited
to certain special places, such as Lourdes in France and Knock in
Ireland, which were officially recognized healing centers.

Needless to say, the power of genuine healings invited the rivalry
of counterfeit healings from the very beginning—as for example, in
the confrontation between St. Paul and the sorcerer Elymas. So it was
not surprising that just as the papacy was corrupted, the officially

recognized saints and healing centers were corrupted in their turn, and soon they were surrounded by all the trappings of religious superstition and energetic buckraking.

Second, the tendency toward specialization and corruption has often led in its turn to an equally common tendency toward overreaction. If the Reformation was right to attempt to reform the many corruptions surrounding the saints and the healing centers, there is no doubt that Reformed people sometimes made the mistake of throwing out the baby along with the bathwater—and dividing the invisible by putting their whole stress on the Word of God at the expense of the Spirit of God. While John Calvin has rightly been called "the theologian of the Holy Spirit," many of his descendants elevated the theory of cessation to the level of a doctrine, and in the process they justly earned the description, "the frozen chosen," for their striking lack of spiritual life and power.

Similarly today, it is common for mainstream Christians to rationalize the dryness of their spiritual state in one of two ways. Some believers still cite the notion of cessation and claim that all forms of spiritual activity ceased after the age of the apostles—when history shows quite clearly that it did not, and Jesus never said it would. Others display a snobbish disdain for all forms of spiritual excess and especially the tales of "the weird, the wild and the wonderful" that flourish at the margins of the church. Holding their noses at anything so indecorous and offensive to their high view of reason and propriety, they shut their eyes to everything to do with the messiness of spiritual reality—and so condemn themselves to prim sterility in a spiritual desert. And all the while the Pentecostal churches and the charismatic renewal movement grow and grow, the fastest growing arm of the global church in the modern era.

Third, if specialization, corruption and overreaction were not enough, there have often been movements of open suppression of the supernatural, when the church has espoused different sets of ideas that have rejected the unseen as unreal and absurd. The doctrine of cessation is one example, later followed by dispensationalism and demythologizing, and such ideas conveniently overlapped with the Enlightenment, whose naturalistic worldview openly dismissed miracles, as thinkers as diverse as David Hume, A. J. Ayer and Richard Dawkins have all made abundantly clear. There was no need for Christians to subscribe to the claims of cessation, dispensationalism, demythologizing or the Enlightenment when to do so was an open betrayal of the faith and philosophically unnecessary to boot. Yet many Christians, such as Rudolf Bultmann, have done so deliberately, and many more have adopted the same attitude unwittingly. Miracles and other supernatural claims about the unseen world are therefore considered fairy tales and quite incredible to modern thinkers.

Modernity provides the capstone to all such trends in its own decisive fashion. Modernism, as a philosophy with its open rationalism, was, is and always will be opposed to faith in God and the supernatural, directly and frontally. But modernity is suaver and more urbane. It has no need of God at all. For who needs God today? As modern people we know how to put a person on the moon. We know how to market a car and sell a perfume or a politician. We know how to grow a church, and the recipe is there for any would-be pastor and church planter to download, from soup to nuts. With our latest science, technology, management and marketing, we have falsified Jesus and the Torah—we now know how to live by bread alone. We have no need of God in any area of life. The entire hypothesis of faith is quite unnecessary. Fear made the gods, says modernism, and shakes its fist. God is no longer necessary, says modernity, and shrugs its shoulders. Modernism had no desire for God, or rather has a strong desire to have no God. Modernity does not even bother with the issue.

In sum, secularization has not meant that religion has disappeared in the modern world. Far from it. But it has meant that for many believers the supernatural has disappeared for all practical purposes from their day-to-day awareness. The unseen has become unreal. Many churches have been lobotomized but carry on as if nothing has changed.

These three crucial shifts are not an exhaustive account of the impact of advanced modernity. They are only broad samples of the damaging trends, and it is up to us to respond with robust and full-bodied Christian faith. For a start, our response should demonstrate a fearless confidence in the gospel. Contrary to the impression I may have created, the impact of modernity is never inevitable. It can and must be resisted so that the church's faith in Jesus demonstrates an integrity and effectiveness that prevails over modernity. But to resist modernity successfully we have to recognize modernity clearly, and that is the task we must tackle with determination today.

In addition, our response must not only trace the broad trends but weigh the specific consequences for different areas of the life of faith. A moment's thought would show, for example, that through pressures such as these, modernity makes evangelism easier, but discipleship harder. Evangelism is easier because modern people are more open to changing faiths than people have ever been (in Peter Berger's words, all the choice and change of today's world mean that modern people are "conversion prone").[12] But discipleship as a "long obedience in the same direction" is against the grain of modern life and infinitely harder. Discipleship for the advanced modern world is an inescapable priority for our time.

Finally, we must hammer home the conclusion that our response requires a Christian account of the world of our day that goes deeper and wider than simply the challenge of ideas. Both modernism and postmodernism raise their own challenges to Christian faith in terms of ideas, but those challenges have largely been covered and are relatively easy to answer. But the challenge of modernity in this wider, fuller sense is one of the defining issues of this century, so it stands as a task for our times that cannot and must not be avoided.

➣ A Prayer ➣

LORD JESUS CHRIST, great Son of God and Lord of all, the entire universe sprang into being at your word, and even death could not hold you down. Forgive our sorry state of worldliness and captivity. Grant that wherever we are shaped by the world rather than by your Word, we may be helped to recognize it and we may be given your power to be freed from it. Grant too that in rising to live as you have called us to live, we may show the world a new and different way of life that once again will free the captives and demonstrate a human way of life that is worthy of you, the author of life and of humanity. Through Jesus Christ our Lord, Amen.

QUESTIONS FOR DISCUSSION

1. Give your own examples of the way in which Christian conviction and commitment has been corrupted to the level of preference. What do you see as the consequences for faith?

2. What would it take to make sure that "Jesus is Lord" covers the whole of life in a fragmented age like ours? Where would you need to think and act more consistently?

3. Is it fair to say that many Christians in the modern world are atheists unawares? Where does the "unseen" and the directly "supernatural" play a part in your life or the life of your church?

chapter three

The War of Spirits

In 1795 Immanuel Kant published one of his last and most influential essays, "Perpetual Peace: A Philosophical Sketch." The theme was not original. Others had written on the same "sweet dream," and Kant took his title after seeing a satirical picture of a graveyard with the words *Pax Perpetua* written over it. But Kant challenged such cynicism, and from his position as the greatest of the Enlightenment philosophers his essay gained an unrivaled prominence and became the opening manifesto of modern peace theory and the movement for international peace studies.

Careful, but audacious and optimistic, the essay represented the epitome of Enlightenment confidence in the power of human reason to shape the future of the world. Jean d'Alembert wrote similarly that "the true system of the world had been recognized," and Diderot claimed that humanity now had the capacity to "put men on the right path."[1] War might be the natural state of humanity, but reason could be so directed as to guide the world toward establishing peace, freedom and harmony. Perpetual peace might be distant, but it was attainable and the trend of world affairs was moving in its direction. Thinkers as different as H. G. Wells and President Woodrow Wilson each owed much to the vision of Kant's essay, as did the rise of later organizations such as the world's mushrooming peace institutes and even the ill-fated League of Nations itself.

Nearly a century later a very different voice sounded out of Germany—passionately frenzied and Dionysian rather than cool and Apollonian. For in 1888, in his last, essay-length book, *Ecce Homo*, Friedrich Nietzsche painted a dramatically contrasting picture of what was to come. Variously interpreted as a super-bombastic self-justification, a satire or the betraying signs of his oncoming madness, he set out to justify and validate himself before the bar of later history. "Why I Am So Wise," he wrote. "Why I Am So Clever," "Why I Write Such Good Books" and "Why I Am a Destiny." "I am not a man. I am dynamite," he claims, for his objective was to blow up all the false pieties that had been mistaken for truth, especially those of religion.

For when the truth squares up to the lie of millennia, we will have upheavals, a spasm of earthquakes, a removal of mountain and valley such as have never been dreamed of. The notion of politics will then completely dissolve into a spiritual war, and all configurations of power from the old society will be exploded—they are all based on a lie: there will be wars such as there have never yet been on earth.[2]

Clearly, Nietzsche is echoing the apocalyptic words of Jesus in the Gospels. Clearly too, he was boasting of being a philosopher in the tradition of Dionysus and his ideal of intoxicated rapture, over against Kant and the philosophers in the tradition of Apollo with their exaltation of cool reason. But beyond the question of Nietzsche's sources and his style, was he right? Was his vision of "spiritual war," which several versions translate as "a war of spirits," accurate? Who had the better insight, Nietzsche or Kant, into the nature of the advanced modern world?

Unquestionably, our world today is closer to Nietzsche's predictions than to Kant's, and no Christian facing the challenges of the twenty-first century can ignore the supernatural dimension of the towering realities we are facing. "Perpetual peace" may have been a powerful aspiration of the world after Kant, but Nietzsche's "war of spirits" has all too often been the brute reality. In other words, in our world in which "everyone is now everywhere," there are no deeper clashes than the conflicts between religions and ideologies, and at their depth (or height) such clashes are rooted in conflicts that go beyond the purely natural, secular or even human. Seen properly, such conflicts are supernatural and even demonic, and this spiritual conflict can be witnessed at three levels above all.

THE ANGEL-PRINCES OF THE NATIONS

The tone deafness of our Western elites is a deficiency that is significant in many different discussions of modern life and serious precisely because they are the ruling elites who dominate modern life in so many ways. The US State Department, for example, has long been known for its heavily secularist view of the world.[3] But for his own personal reasons, President Obama led the blind and stubborn folly of his entire administration in refusing to name the plainly obvious role of radical Islam in Middle Eastern violence by insisting on calling it only "violent extremism."

Obama's obtuseness had several roots, including his personal background, but as I have noted repeatedly, a common feature of many of our leaders is that they are "unmusical" (Max Weber). They simply do not hear the "music of the spheres" (Albert Einstein) by which most people in the world orchestrate their lives. They live in the "world without windows" (Peter Berger) that we looked at in the last chapter. Like the cave dwellers in Plato's famous parable, their sense of reality goes no farther than the flickering shadows on the walls of the cave, and they have never seen the sun. Indeed, confusing their myopic attention span with the limits of ultimate reality, they have fallen for the conclusion that what they do not see

or hear is not there to be seen and heard, and not there at all—
which even Nietzsche called the "acoustic illusion" that any dog, bat
or bear could falsify in a second.

For such people, Nietzsche's notion of a "war of spirits" would
be illusory and delusional, and the term would be seen merely as a
synonym for "extreme intensity." To be sure, Nietzsche himself was
an atheist, but he was Dionysian rather than Apollonian, and there
are some leading intellectuals today who are like him. They do not
believe in God, but they speak of the "daemonic" as more than a
metaphor. The daemonic for them is a higher form of sublime in-
tuition or even a possession by some outside force. The daemonic
as they see it goes beyond the ordinary perception of most people,
and it has to be grasped by more than reason, but it is still within
the realm of the natural.

Needless to say, even that view falls far short of the Jewish and
Christian understanding of spiritual warfare. In the ringing story
of Jewish freedom in the book of Exodus, when Moses cries out,
"Let my people go!" the famous contest is not so much between
Moses and Pharaoh as between the Lord and the gods of Egypt—
including the god Apis, whose bull-calf image was cast in gold.
Centuries later, as Nebuchadnezzar, Babylon's great captain of
history, comes to discover through his own dramatic experience,
"*It is* Heaven *that* rules" (Dan 4:26). But heaven's power to rule
prevails in the course of a war that is waged in heaven as well as on
earth. The archangel Michael's victory on behalf of God's people,
the Jews, is a victory in a very real battle against the very real angel-
princes of Persia and Greece—and by extension, the very real
angel-princes of Rome, Madrid, Paris, Amsterdam, London and all
the other succeeding powers of history, right down to Washington,
Moscow and Beijing today.

You can judge a culture by what it talks about and what it refuses
to talk about, and talk of "spiritual warfare" would be a useful litmus

test today. As theologian Walter Wink observes, "Angels, spirits, principalities, powers, gods, Satan—these, along with other spiritual realities, are the unmentionables of our culture. The dominant materialistic worldview has absolutely no place for them." They are archaic relics of a primitive past because "modern secularism simply has no categories, no vocabulary, no presuppositions by which to discern what it was in the actual experience of people that brought these words to speech."[4] Even supporters of Nietzsche reduce his term "war of spirits" to a vivid metaphor.

To Wink's credit, he opened up the topic again for theology, but his position falls far short of the biblical understanding. In fact, he argues that the biblical worldview is "beyond being salvaged, limited as it was by the science, philosophy and religion of its age."[5] As he interprets the term "power and principalities," all institutions have two sides, an outer structure and an inner spirit, so the term is simply a way of describing the inner spirit of an institution. Principalities and powers are therefore "an intrinsic spirituality, an inner essence, a collective culture or ethos, which cannot be directly deciphered from its outer manifestations."[6] They are not transcendent realities but merely a "symbolic projection" because that was the only language available to people in more primitive times. Thus all powers have this dual aspect. They have an outer and visible form, which includes leaders, magistrates, police officers and offices, and an inner and invisible form, which provides them with legitimacy, compliance and clout.

Illuminating though Wink's description is at that reduced level, the Jewish and Christian Scriptures go much further. If sin is evil at the personal level, principalities and powers are evil at the cosmic level. They are not merely human projections or a way of describing the inner spirit of an institution. They are independent supernatural realities that transcend the natural plane of our human experience. Thus there are not only two cities in the world—the City of God and the City of Man, as St. Augustine taught. There are two kingdoms in the universe—the kingdom of God and light and the kingdom of Satan and darkness—as Jesus taught and demonstrated by his confrontations and healings. If we are members of one kingdom, we are automatically and emphatically opposed to the other, and there is a war between them going on all the time.

Derek Prince, the Cambridge-educated philosopher and Bible teacher who drew not only from the Bible's teaching but his personal experience at the Battle of El Alamein and afterwards, came to his own settled conviction: "Human history is truly explained by the interplay between these forces."[7] "Do You not know," Pilate said to Jesus, "that I have authority to release You, and I have authority to crucify You?" (Jn 19:10). He was incredulous that a mere Galilean peasant did not seem to appreciate what was at stake in the way he answered back to the Roman governor. But Jesus' next words must have angered as well as stunned him, for they soared above any perceived cheek or stupidity to make an assertion that, if not true, was a sure symptom of delusion as well as an insult to mighty Rome. Addressing the chosen representative of the mightiest power on the earth of his day, and almost any day, Jesus calmly replied, "You would have no authority over Me, unless it had been given you from above" (Jn 19:11).

That one sentence surely merits an hour of worship and reflection. At the very least it means that nothing short of an insistence that "principalities and powers" are independent supernatural realities, and that God rules over them all, can make sense of the biblical account of the nations and their power. For in the biblical account nations are powerful, independent realities that shape the people within them. Hence the old maxim, "That which chooses the chooser determines the choice." But nations, and not only individuals, too, have fallen. For Adam and Eve, disobedience led to exclusion. And for nations, as shown in the account of the Tower

of Babel, disobedience led to confusion. So as the Bible's story unfolds, it is said that nations can become idols, and nations too will
be judged. At the last day, even the great city, St. Augustine's City
of Man, will be judged, "for in one hour she has been laid waste!"
(Rev 18:19). But that is not the whole story, and there is good news
for nations too. Nations too may be redeemed, and at the great day
at the end of time "ALL THE NATIONS WILL COME AND WORSHIP
BEFORE YOU" (Rev 15:4).

Developing this grand view of human and international affairs,
Martin Buber explored the depth of the darkness of the early days
of World War II in 1941. Every nation, he argued, has its own pre-
siding spirit and genius, its "prince" or its "god." It worships its own
innermost essence as its idol. The secularist state is therefore a blas-
phemous state, but it cannot last. For the national idol, titanic
though it may seem in its time, develops, expands and then always
overreaches and dies. Its god is simply not God, and it cannot be.
The nation of Israel, in contrast, was chosen directly by God, and
its calling as a nation was to worship God truly and so to witness
to the truth of the one true God to the nations.

Unbeknownst to Buber, Hitler was planning the "final solution"
at the precise moment the great Jewish philosopher was writing.
Israel's very existence called the nations into question, so in the
explosive words that George Steiner, a Jew himself, put into Hitler's
mouth, "There had to be a solution, a *final solution*."[8] The Jews were
the ultimate "impossible people," so their very being was an affront
to what was then the ultimate pagan and idolatrous power of the
day. God's chosen people had to be eliminated and their witness
silenced. Did not Nietzsche foresee the same absolute necessity to
kill God himself, for he saw clearly that the "death of God" was not
a casual event or an accident but a "murder"? "But he . . . *had* to die.
. . . He *always* saw me: I wanted to have revenge on such a witness—
or to no longer live myself. The God who saw everything, *everyone*

included—this God had to die! A person cannot stand it, that such a witness should live."[9]

Wink comments on Buber's essay, "When the national spirit decays and disintegrates, and the nation turns its face to nothingness instead of participating in the whole, it is on the verge of death."[10] As we survey the world today, is it not increasingly clear that nothing short of this same insistence will make sense of the cataclysmic conflicts of our time and of the decadence of the West? Yet we have lost any sense of "nation gods," the "angel princes" of countries or the idea that there will be a judgment of the nations. All that is left of these titanic notions in our puny thinking is the soft, sweet, sentimental idea of guardian angels over the beds of children. It will not be easy to recover the gigantic scale of the biblical view. But we have to start by acknowledging that even when we seek to do justice to it, our understanding of this dimension is severely limited, and many of those who have taken it seriously have spun off in bizarre directions. In short, the perils of our misunderstanding the powers, or responding to them in wrong ways, are legion.

To argue whether these powers are *above, behind* or *beyond* the realties we see is surely to miss the point too. These terms are all spatial, as is our human understanding on the natural plane, so it is incapable of expressing the precise realities that are beyond our understanding. But whatever and wherever the principalities and powers finally are, the point is that they are real. Daniel was told about the angel-princes of Persia and Greece and a twenty-one-day war in heaven, the kings of both Judah and Israel were assessed by their actions in approving or removing the "high places" that represented pagan spiritual powers, Jesus spoke of the evil one and the need to disarm a strong man before raiding his house, and St. Paul wrote of the power of the cross in disarming the powers of darkness and of his own strategy of demolishing strongholds that proudly defied a knowledge of God. Dare we say it? The spirit of the age is not a metaphor, and it cannot be overcome by action and argument alone.

In our world without windows, all such references would be dismissed as delusional, so once again the question is truth and adequacy. Are such descriptions true? Is history best understood, explained and lived out on a purely natural plane, or does the full range of historical reality require an account and a strategy that at times transcends the natural and the secular altogether? (For George Washington, the "invisible hand" in the American revolution was not the "invisible hand" of Adam Smith's market place, but the unmistakable providence of God in action.) The biblical answer to that question is in no doubt. In, behind and above titanic powers such as human empires and ideologies, there are dark supernatural powers at work and opposed to the kingdom of our Lord. We will never explain reality or prevail against the opposition if we engage only on the natural plane of reality. There is not only an unseen world beyond the seen, but time and again the real battle is in the unseen world—a war in heaven. Those who win the battle in the heavens are the decisive factor in the course of history.

WORLD ORDER AND THE IDOLATRY OF NATIONS

This titanic clash of supernatural powers needs to be thought through by Christians at many levels today, but especially three. The first is at the level of world powers and international relations. The "nations" are of course one of the recognized supernatural realities in the Bible, as when Daniel is told of the angel-princes of the superpowers of his day. But what does such a notion mean? It is common to distinguish patriotism as a natural and legitimate love of one's place and one's country, from nationalism as a dangerous idolatry of one's nation. But the distinction is far harder to maintain in practice. Nations, after all, are countries, and their role in unifying diverse religious, ethnic and linguistic groups can be highly beneficial. Think of the brilliant success of America's original motto, *E pluribus unum*, or the importance of the European Union slogan, "Unity Out of Diversity." There is truth, then, in the old aphorism: "Nationalism is patriotism disliked, and patriotism is nationalism liked."

There is no question that idolatry is the key to the danger of both, for both countries and nations can become gods when they are inflated and put in God's place. This is especially so when the nations are led by leaders and by states whose universalist ideology is not balanced by particularism, so that it is inflated as "the truth of all times and all peoples," whether Marxism, National Socialism, democracy, capitalism or Islam. Any such truth must be advanced, imposed on all others and defended at all costs, and as the last century underscores in blood-red letters, millions of human beings may be slaughtered in the name of promoting or defending such gods. If the world ever comes close to destroying the earth and large swathes of humanity with it, it will doubtless be in defense of the interests of some universalist ideology or another that is too important not to be defended to the death—of others. (Sadly, to our undying shame, we Christians must confess that in the long Catholic centuries Christians promoted the Christian faith in just such a way, thus overriding freedom of conscience and the free and voluntary worship that God loves and calls for.)

A conundrum arises for those who dismiss principalities and powers as a delusion. Like Christians, they believe in idols and rightly deride and dismiss them as natural realities worshiped falsely as gods. But unlike Christians, they do not believe in gods—for Christians believe that "gods" are spiritual forces that are supernatural realities, but they are not God. There is no God but God. The outcome, then, as Wink states, is that "when a nation is made a god *it becomes a god*."[11] It becomes the worship of the nation itself, and when this is absolutized it unleashes a mass devotion that is false, idolatrous and truly demonic. How else could secular Western nations that would never admit to believing in gods of any kind end by sacrificing human lives on a scale worthy of the blood-thirstiest pagans? John Bull and Uncle Sam appear no more threatening than the beautiful goddess of Athens, Athena. But tell that to the citizens of Melos, Cologne, Dresden, Hiroshima and Nagasaki when the destruction of the innocents was the price paid by the nations who defended themselves by destroying others in the name of their incontrovertible ideologies.

HOW MANY SUNS IN THE GLOBAL SKY?

Take, for instance, the present urgency of the search for a world order to suit the global era. The broad current possibilities for such a world order are plain, though just to set them out shows how difficult it is to attain peace, harmony and stability under modern conditions, and how far we are from having leaders with such astuteness and such high objectives in mind. In short, the global era makes the search for world order both more urgent and more daunting than ever. Is it fanciful or a delusion to think of the clash of unseen powers, each with a will and a supernatural force of its own?

One possibility for the future is that the entire world will move in the direction of the long dominant European system that grew out of the Peace of Westphalia in 1648. This was based on the notion of equilibrium and a carefully calculated balancing between the power of separate sovereign states, which broadly recognize the rule of law and respect for noninterference in each other's sovereignty. But such a system is no foregone conclusion, for where are the great statesmen-balancers such as Metternich, Canning, Bismarck and Kissinger who could make it possible? The two world wars of the twentieth century have already shown the fragility of this system, and the balancing required in the global era may prove too dizzying a feat for the myopic politicians of our day, especially under the turbulent conditions of advanced modernity. And Europe, of course, which pioneered the Westphalian model, has effectively abandoned it already in its search for a new supranational and transcontinental unity beyond the reality of its diverse states—in other words, its search for a novel utopian empire of peace.

The second possibility is that with the faltering of Western dominance and of liberal democracy, one of history's most ancient and natural trends will reemerge, but this time with global pretensions that dwarf any of its previous forms: the rise of an advanced modern world empire or even of more than one competing empire. Empires have been far too common a form of human government for any but democratic ideologues to miss. But does the global era reopen the door to the mad dream of the entire world under a single ideology, a single market or a single empire? If that were to happen, might it be a Chinese empire seeking to absorb "all under heaven" in the smothering embrace of its authoritarian state and its burgeoning economy? Or could it be a nuclear-armed radical Islamic empire, seeking to expand the "house of Islam" globally and to recapture the splendor of an Ottoman-style caliphate on a far larger and grander stage of history?

There was a rash of such millennial talk in the mid-sixteenth century during the clash between Christendom and Islam. Erasmus wrote of the Ottoman ruler's well-known bid for "the great prize," becoming "the monarch of the world . . . for the world cannot any longer bear to have two suns in the sky."[12] Sultan Suleiman the Magnificent was equally forthright himself: "Just as there is only one God in heaven there can be only one empire on earth."[13] Will tomorrow's Middle Eastern rulers be any more tolerant of two suns in the global sky? The present religious leaders of Iran have openly talked of their vision to revive the caliphate and expand its dominance around the world, as have many more of the Muslim radicals, including the seemingly delusional leader of the barbarous Islamic State. Why do we ignore the long clear lessons of history and do not take "Death to America!" "Death to Israel!" and "Death to Britain!" either literally or seriously?

The third possibility is that a harbinger of the future of the world can be seen in the steady proliferation of nuclear-armed states, in the spread of collapsing states such as Syria and Libya, and in the cataclysm of terrorism and barbarism that is now convulsing the Middle East. Needless to say, that possibility would make a mockery of any notion of world order and take the world far closer to Hobbes's "war of all against all." But what if the recent convulsions in the Middle East were to be replicated elsewhere—for example, if Russian powermongering were to make the Baltic region more like the Balkans? The warnings are plain. With the savage and wanton destruction of human life, the terrible displacement of thousands of wandering migrants, the grim production of the overcrowded "nowherevilles" of the refugee camps, and the barbaric destruction of the traces of ancient art and civilization, the world could be facing a mounting crisis of humanity that would stagger the moral imagination and beggar the best intentions of the ablest leaders.

Will the cool, scientific reason of our brave new atheists pick up where Kant left off and guide the world safely toward perpetual peace? Or is it more likely that we will witness power and evil on a scale that defies all reason and science and unleashes a lawlessness and malevolence that cries out to heaven itself for explanation and redress? History tells us already that the spirit of nations can outweigh the mightiest armaments of an opposing enemy. How else could tiny Greece have defeated mighty Persia in the fifth century BC, or North Vietnam prevail against the overwhelming military power of the United States in the twentieth century? At the very least we cannot afford the stupidity and shallowness of American presidents, European prime ministers and other world leaders who dare not name the names of the religions and ideologies in question. The twentieth century made war itself costly beyond all calculations and nuclear war unimaginable. But the day may well be near when the war of spirits of both Nietzsche and, more importantly, the Hebrew and Christian Scriptures will no longer be a metaphor but a terrible reality.

HIGH PLACES IN THE PUBLIC SQUARE

The public squares of our world are the second sphere where the war of spirits must be explored. From the celebrated Greek agora below the Acropolis in Athens to the forum in Rome, to the Houses of Parliament in London, and to the US Congress in Washington DC, and their many equivalents in other countries, the notion of the public square has been prized in the Western world. It is the place where citizens and their leaders can come together to debate and decide the issues of common public life. Once referring to a physical place, the term *public square* expanded to be a metaphor that included any place where issues of common pubic life were debated—such as the op-ed pages of a newspaper or a talk show on the radio or television. Now, in the age of the Internet, the term has expanded yet again and become virtual, so that we can talk of a very rudimentary but nevertheless real global public square.

Needless to say, the ideal of the common good and a common vision of the good of all was at the heart of the notion of the public square in any of these forms. But the steady expansion of the idea of the public square has not been matched by an equal expansion of the civility needed to advance the common good and negotiate the explosively expanded diversity of individuals and groups who now have easy access to the public square. The result is the emergence of a culture war in many nations, which makes a mockery of both civility and the common good. And once again such culture wars surely have a hidden dimension that is another front in the wider war of spirits, for at their root the crux issue of any nation's culture war is authority. Whose faiths, ideals and ideas have the authority to shape the foundations of the nation's life?

Our current notion of a culture war goes back to nineteenth-century Germany and the culture war, or *kulturkampf*, waged between Chancellor Otto von Bismarck and the Roman Catholic Church. The decade long "struggle for the dominance in culture" centered on Bismarck's attempt to subject the Church to state controls. He himself was an ardent Protestant, and though the papacy was at a low ebb in terms of political power, he feared that the promulgation of papal infallibility in 1870 would give it fresh impetus to revive and assert its dominance and set back his vision of a German empire. Nearly a decade of conflict in areas such as education and marriage proved fruitless, and Bismarck eventually retreated, conceding that his measures had only served to stiffen the opposition.

In the case of America's present culture war, the issues go far deeper, the divisions have gone far wider, and the struggle has lasted far longer—half a century and counting. The outcome leaves the United States as deeply divided—politically, economically, racially, culturally and religiously—as at any point except for the Civil War. Either the Supreme Court decision in the Everson case in 1947 or Madalyn Murray O'Hair's lawsuits against school prayer in the early 1960s are taken as the first shots in the struggle. But an endless list of conflicts and lawsuits have followed, including clashes over the Ten Commandments, public prayers and Christmas carols. Supremely, of course, the two most explosive flashpoints in the ongoing battles have been abortion and marriage.

One prominent feature of the impact of the Internet has been the progressive abandonment of civility and the rise of flash mobs, smearing, bullying and intimidation, often from the side of the newly illiberal liberalism. This has provided one more impetus to the gathering realization that freedom and democracy, far from blood brothers as many people claimed blithely in the George W. Bush era, are clearly beginning to go in opposite directions. But in all the struggles, two dominant issues have raised their heads again and again: the place of religions in American society and the understanding of how religions and public life should be related. It is clear that the three overlapping forces mentioned earlier—the philosophy of secularism, the process of secularization and the public policy of strict separationism—have in effect converged to become the default position of the American elite.

In the process these forces have slowly become dominant and increasingly intolerant, and there is no question that the only serious obstacle in their path is the Christian church. The result is another factor aiding the cut-flower civilization set out in the introduction. America never was a Christian nation in any formal or established sense, but there is no question that the Christian faith was the faith of most Americans at the beginning, and that Jewish and Christian ideals underlie most of the distinctive values for which America at its best has been known worldwide.

Should the struggle end where the state of the culture war is now, it would be clear that the America the world once knew would have gone, though the full dimensions of the newly victorious forces would not yet be clear. It is in that sense that America is post-Christian, but not yet fully non-Christian.

It is a mistake to think that the vast changes wrought by the culture war affect religion and religious people only, for many other things have been touched, including freedom itself and America's way of handling diversity. In his stirring "Memorial and Remonstrance," James Madison described the American way of handling deep religious and ideological differences as the "true remedy" to a problem that has spilled rivers of human blood. The remedy was never perfect, of course, but in neglecting it and then rejecting it without understanding its genius, Americans have squandered their own rich heritage and chosen the model of the French Revolution rather than their own.

Once again, is it fanciful or delusional to see the culture war as partly spiritual warfare and to reject the idea that it can be fought on a purely natural plane and with purely secular weapons? There was an old Evangelical maxim that "the Lord's work must always be done in the Lord's way to receive the Lord's blessing." But "the Lord's way" surely means that not only must we return good for evil and love for hate as we oppose our "enemies" in public life, but that we wage war powerfully and appropriately against the unseen forces of darkness just as Jesus did.

WAR IN THE CAMP OF THE PEOPLE OF GOD

The third sphere where we need to think through the place of spiritual warfare is in the church itself. Most incredibly of all, the authority of Jesus and the Scriptures has been called into question within the camp of God's people almost as much as outside in the culture. Neither authority nor tradition have ever held the place in American hearts that they had in many European countries. The American republic, after all, was founded on an emphatic rejection of monarchy as well as of tradition and the old ways of doing things. The American project was hailed as the new order of the ages (*novus ordo seclorum*), and it was created by intention and by ideas. But even the general regard for authority that was once there has diminished over time, hurried on its way by grand disillusioning scandals such as Watergate and reinforced by the relentless schooling in mistrust, suspicion and cynicism that is the bitter residue of postmodernism.

"We have no king but Jesus" was the original cry of Christian republicans who believed in the kingdom of heaven alongside the republic on earth. But since then, the sense of republicanism has grown and that of kingship has diminished, just as the founders' ordered freedom has given way to libertarianism, so that in effect the truth now is that "we have no king but ourselves." And as in the days of the Hebrew judges, this means in practice that there is no king in Israel and "everyone [does] what [is] right in his own eyes" (see Judg 21:25). Personal reasons, individual interests, subjective choices, private agendas and fashionable trends are what really decide the issues of the day for many people in America's "anything goes" culture. Sometimes the collapse of authority leads to the cheekily defiant "Mistrust authority" of the bumper stickers. Equally it can result in a quiet, amiable and soft-centered accommodationism to whatever are the prevailing winds of fashionable opinion blowing in on Christians from the wider culture.

Adjusting and accommodating to external pressure can take many different forms, including resignation, withdrawal, passivity and quietism. And these in turn will depend on how severe the pressure has been and how long it has been applied. But whatever the situation the church finds itself in, accommodation usually means that the first news of liberation will be met with skepticism and mistrust—as Moses and Aaron discovered when they approached the elders of Israel with the news of the Lord's liberation from Pharaoh. At such a time, the biblical assertion of authority will come across as provocative and utterly absurd to those it challenges: "Who is the Lord that I should obey his voice to let Israel go?" (Ex 5:2). To those inside the church, the same declaration of authority will be inconvenient and deeply unsettling, for the status quo has been declared no longer acceptable.

But the issue cannot be sugarcoated. Authority is central, uncompromising and inescapable for Christians. For those who follow Jesus, the Christian faith is not primarily a philosophy, a worldview, an ethic or a lifestyle. It is all those things but more because of the authority of Jesus. To believe in Jesus is to bow twice and then to obey forever, as Francis Schaeffer put it. When we could not discover God by ourselves, he disclosed himself, so we bow once to his revelation. When we could not rescue ourselves by ourselves, he saved us, so we bow again to his redemption. In other words, we may be very aware of our part in searching for God and all that it meant and cost us, and we are certainly aware that the step of faith is our wholehearted responsibility, just as it is a fully warranted conviction of truth. We are never more completely ourselves than when we make that decision to trust in God.

Yet that step is always more a matter of grace than achievement. Its good news is the story of God's reaching down to us, rather than our rising to God. As C. S. Lewis expressed it famously, it is the story of the cat catching the mouse and not the other way around. But then, once we have been convinced unreservedly that his claims are true and Jesus is Lord, we go forward to follow him and live in the light of that truth and under the lordship of that claim. So the way of Jesus is constituted by the authority of Jesus and lived out under that authority. Jesus is Lord, and he is Lord of every last part of our lives and Lord until our very last breath. We are not following a good suggestion, pursuing our right to happiness or choosing a way of life that appears to pay richer dividends. We have been called by God, and we are under his authority. Thus to follow teaching other than the teaching of Jesus is anathema (accursed), St. Paul says. To stray from his lordship and abandon his way means shipwreck. Conformity in many areas of life is boring, but conformity to the will and the way of Jesus is life and freedom itself—under his authority.

Perhaps most amazingly of all, our Lord and Master himself was not only authoritative but under authority too. True, he claimed his own absolute and unqualified authority when he spoke and acted, which stunned the crowds and provoked the authorities of the day.

True, he unequivocally confirmed and strengthened the Jewish reverence toward the Scriptures as the supreme authority as the Word of God. But strikingly, he who was the supreme authority for his followers submitted to the authority of his Father and to the Word himself—to his own cost.

This costly submission can be seen when Jesus was tempted by the evil one in the wilderness, and he refused the devil's allures because he was submitting to the Word. The account shows that he not only quoted the Word as a weapon against the devil ("It is written" [Lk 4:4]), but that he followed the Word as a way of life and rejected the devil's spectacular alternative offers. The same point is clearer and costlier still in the Garden of Gethsemane, when Jesus submitted to what the Scriptures had said *had to happen*, rather than sidestepping the cross as almost everything in him wished to do. ("Father, if it is possible, let this cup pass from Me; yet not as I will, but as You will" [Mt 26:39].) For Jesus, what the Scriptures said, God himself said, and that was the end of the matter. He only spoke, he said, "just as the Father has told Me" (Jn 12:50). And so he suffered and died too.

No picture comes closer to expressing the lordship and authority of Jesus than St. John's repeated use of the word *Pantocrator* in the Book of Revelation. As any tourist to Greece and Turkey knows, this is an image that was resonant and beloved in early Christian art and history. The word combines two Greek words that together express Christ's almighty and all-encompassing rule. Jesus Christ rules over all the world, he sustains all the world and he judges all the world. In our little lives, we only live, breathe, think and act under this supreme authority.

With such an awesome Lord and such a clear and costly example of his own attitude to authority, how can it be that so many Christians reject this sublime authority so casually? How can they turn aside from this wholehearted submission to assert their own preferences and never even tremble? How can so many now believe—as the opinion surveys claim to show—that they now regard Jesus as *a* way, *a* truth and *a* life, rather than "the way, and the truth, and the life" (Jn 14:6)? And how can it be that certain Christians loudly profess that they continue to hold to a "high view of biblical authority," yet reject its clear, enduring teaching when it so clearly suits them, say, over the justification of homosexual marriage? What are we to make of their interpretations, with so many spurious arguments from silence, such brazen special pleading and all toward the end of so much obviously self-interested, self-justifying sinful behavior?

The greatest scholars of our age, liberal and not only conservative, along with the united voices of the greatest scholars of all the ages, have shown beyond all reasonable doubt that the Bible is plainly opposed to homosexual behavior, just as it is to all heterosexual sexual behavior outside of marriage—and they are confirmed in their conclusion by the majority of homosexual scholars themselves. Yet our brave new Christians trust in their own brilliant reinterpretations and serve their own interests without a qualm. Thomas Jefferson trembled when he pondered on slavery and remembered that God was just. It is surely time for some Christians to tremble when we read and hear the casual twisting and discarding of Scripture by those who still claim to be faithful. There is a rottenness in the church that must be addressed. Christians too need to return and stand humbly and obediently with all their fellow believers before the lordship and authority of Jesus Pantocrator, ruler, sustainer and judge of all the world.

Needless to say, today's revisionism is no new path. Protestant liberals have blazed the revisionist road for two centuries and more, and look where it has taken them. Many have addressed this crisis in detail, so it needs no further elaboration here.[14] The extremes of Protestant liberal revisionism have quite simply committed spiritual, theological and institutional suicide, and no one who follows them now can claim to be innocent with a straight face. Evangelicals were once known for their robust and defining view of the authority of the Word, as set out for example in J. I. Packer's classic *Fundamentalism and the Word of God*. In fact, they were once almost defined as nonliberals in direct contrast to such revisionism. But the last generation has seen a significant wing of Evangelicalism—some emergent Evangelicals, some seeker-sensitive extremists, some relevance-chasing hipster pastors—set out to revise, reinterpret and eventually abandon the faith with the same suicidal, lemming-like folly.

Yet most probably the greatest danger in the coming generations will not be in the extremes but in the soft center of the almost-anything-goes, amiable accommodationism of current Evangelicalism. As in the time of the prophet Elijah, the postmodern church has become a breeding ground for the undecided, for fence sitters, for people who want to have their cake and eat it too, and so for syncretists who have forgotten the meaning of the word. There are too many Christians weary of taking a stand because they are so wary of repeating the mistakes of the past. They have become "whatever" people, those who hedge their bets and watch from the sidelines to see who will win the contest on the Mount Carmels of our day.

Doubtless, new terms will be coined to describe them, and old terms such as *neo* this and *neo* that will become common again, but they will all be unconvincing and unsatisfactory. "Follower of Jesus," "Christian" (and when appropriate "Evangelical," "Catholic" and "Orthodox") are quite enough when biblically defined. Unless today's spiritual and theological half-way houses are challenged and resolved, they will become like doubts—either they are resolved and lead back to an even more robust faith or they will slip and slide until they crash down to full-blown disbelief.

For some time now it has been said that those who are faithful to Christ in each denomination are closer to those who are also faithful in other denominations than they are to the members of their own denomination who are revisionists. Along with the melting of denominational differences, this fact has lent a powerful momentum toward a new and welcome Christian unity between all who confess that Jesus Christ is Lord. But it also serves to highlight the contrast of the deadly menace of Christian revisionism, whether Protestant liberal, Roman Catholic or Evangelical. As I said, St. Paul underscored the seriousness of preaching "another gospel" by pronouncing it "accursed," and Kierkegaard added his own heavy condemnation in calling such revisionists "kissing Judases"—those who betray Jesus with an interpretation. The war of spirits has invaded even the camp of the people of God, and as in the story of Moses and Phinehas responding to Israel's revelries around the golden calf, it is time to see who is on the Lord's side—and who, through their own decisions, chooses not to be and to rebel. The lordship and authority of God and the very meaning and survival of Christian faith and its integrity are at stake.

For Christians who ponder the extraordinary condition of the modern world, two things are surely undeniable. One is that Nietzsche's "war of spirits" is a far closer depiction of contemporary realities than Kant's "perpetual peace," and the other is that we cannot respond to the madness and evil of what is going on without taking the biblical account of reality seriously. There are unseen supernatural forces at work. Such an understanding may be plainest in the cataclysmic convulsions created by Islamic extremism in the Middle East, the enormous tensions created by the decline of America, the rise of ancient but reborn China and the faltering of the utopian European project. But it is also apparent in the contentious controversies in the public life of many countries and even in the quarrels and divisions within the church of God. Ours is a time when cultures are roiling, nations are in uproar, civilizations themselves appear to be heaving, cracking and crumbling, and no one who ignores the wars of spirit can either understand or respond to our world.

Nietzsche's hoped-for outcome of the spiritual warfare was the rise of superhumans, a grand revaluation of all values and triumph in the war of "Dionysus against the Crucified." In the face of the same global realities, Kant argued that "perpetual peace" would come in one of two ways: either as the achievement of human reason or as the fruit of a weariness that followed some momentous catastrophe that left no other choice than resigned cooperation.

We who follow Jesus would part company with both philosophers. Nietzsche's option has been stained indelibly by its Nazi incarnation, though it will doubtless rise again in a new form. Kant's option is too utopian, though its dream will prove enduring and seductive. Our view of history and the world is different. God is Creator of the cosmos and the Lord of history. It is heaven that rules. Our Lord has the whole world in his strong, good hands, and the ultimate outcome will not be decided by the "invisible hand" of the market or by the "Leviathan" of the modern state, but by the management of God that we count on as providence. In sum, the great cosmic contest of history is real. The war of spirits is real, very real, and our part is not to fear but to trust, to watch—and (as we shall see) to take our small but significant parts in this wider war of spirits.

⇒ A Prayer ⇐

OUR FATHER, ALL POWER in heaven and earth is yours. Mightier than our mightiest power, more awesome than our most terrifying visions, we bow before your majesty, we rest in your covenant faithfulness, and we confess our folly in trusting in any power except your own. Open our eyes that we may see all you want us to know of the unseen realities of your kingdom. Cleanse our hearts that our motives may be your glory and not simply our human good. Grant us a healthy awareness of the powers of darkness but an even healthier knowledge of the power of your Spirit. And if it be your gracious will, fill us with your power and use us to your glory, not for our sake but for yours. Through Jesus Christ our Lord, Amen.

QUESTIONS FOR DISCUSSION

1. To what extent are you, your family and your local church "tone deaf" and "unmusical"? Why do you think so much of the Western church is not enjoying the fulfillment of all that Jesus promised to his disciples when he left the earth and gave us his Spirit?

2. How do we enter into all that Jesus promised his followers without going overboard with "the weird, the wild and the wonderful"?

3. What difference would it make practically to take seriously the idea of "principalities and powers" behind world events?

chapter four

Exploring the
Heart of Darkness

S ome years ago I was invited to speak to a group of representa-
tives in the US Congress, and at the end of my talk a congressman put up his hand.

"A small boy can put his finger in a dike, and be a hero," he said,
obviously referring to the celebrated story of the flood in the Netherlands. "But when I look out around America, what I see is a mudslide. What can anyone do about that?"

The answer of course is not much. Mudslides collapse, gush, flow,
batter, drown and then seep everywhere, and their big debris flows
of mud, rocks and trees are almost unstoppable, carrying everything
before them in their destructive path. If the problems we face were
few and unrelated, that would be one thing. If they were just a matter
of economics, say, or technology, education, crime or immigration
by themselves, we could deal with them singly. There could be a
fabled silver bullet. We live in the great age of technology, and where
there are discrete problems, there are always experts to solve the
different problems. Nothing is easier today than to call on the expert,
the specialist, the consultant, the pollster or the pundit, and have
them fix it or give us a full explanation (and the bill).

One reason for this mudslide effect is the understanding that in the global era all problems have multicausal explanations and all have become interconnected in their turn—giving rise to the saying that "everything is interconnected and no one is in charge." Obvious to us today, this point was one of the insights behind the founding of the celebrated global think tank the Club of Rome in 1968, which Aurelio Peccei, the founder, called the new "predicament of mankind."[1] There are no longer separate political, economic or social problems. So it no longer works to pinpoint individual problems and propose individual solutions—"each problem is related to every other problem; each apparent solution to a problem may aggravate or interfere with others."[2] The global era demands that leaders think globally, multicausally and holistically, and respect the entire ecology of human ideas, values and institutions, nations, and the earth itself.

That is certainly true, but I will argue in this chapter that there is an even deeper reason for the mudslide effect. So the congressman was unquestionably correct. Our present problems appear to be more like a mudslide or the spread of toxic mold or a poison gas. The devastation and the damage seem to have gone everywhere, and they have touched and ruined everything. There is no silver bullet to hand. As the psalmist wrote centuries ago, "If the foundations are destroyed, / What can the righteous do?" (Ps 11:3). Or as the old nursery rhyme says of Humpty Dumpty's fall from the wall: "All the king's horses and all the king's men couldn't put Humpty together again."

Such talk raises several questions: What is the mudslide, culturally speaking? What are the factors that cause the seemingly unstoppable erosion and collapse? What are the ideas and events that saturate such bedrock solidities as faith and the family until they no longer hold? What are the policies that damage things once considered massive and unmovable until they suddenly shift, slide and collapse, with nothing that can be done except to follow the path of devastation? Other people prefer different metaphors, such as cultural *fraying* or *unraveling*, but they too raise the question of what and why the erosion, the fraying or the unraveling is happening.

Another powerful and helpful term is *crisis of cultural authority*. It is used to shine light on the way in which ideas and ideals that were once fresh and powerful in a society come to lose their compelling power. A *crisis of legitimacy* is another term that seeks to express the same point. But the question for all such terms is why? What exactly lies behind them? Only God knows the full story of all the causes and interconnections that make such crises happen. But having thought about the problem and explored it from many angles for many years, I would put forward three different but separately powerful trends that in the case of the United States are causing the cultural damage, the middle one being at the heart of the mudslide effect. These trends are slightly different in other countries, but they are clearest in the United States because, for the time being, America is still the lead nation in the modern world.

THE COMPLETEST REVOLUTION OF ALL

The first trend is the deliberate and systematic rejection of the foundational place of the Jewish and Christian roots of American society. The story of the rejection of the Christian faith in the West is well known, particularly as told from the standpoint of beliefs and ideas. And the place of seminal anti-Christian thinkers, from Nietzsche and Bertrand Russell to Richard Dawkins, Christopher Hitchens and Sam Harris, is well known too. But the assault on beliefs is too often considered in a vacuum, as if it were a matter of philosophy and a crisis of faith only, whereas it needs to be placed in its wider setting in culture, and tracing its longer-term significance for the West.

Consider the same repudiation from another angle. Lord James Bryce was the British ambassador to the United States in the first decade of the twentieth century, and because of his classic book *The American Commonwealth*, he is often considered second only to Alexis de Tocqueville as the most astute foreign commentator on America. A strong liberal, he was similar to Tocqueville, who was famous for recognizing the prime national importance of religion in the American political order and especially the Christian faith. Bryce was equally emphatic: "Christianity is in fact understood to be, though not legally the established religion, yet the national religion."[3]

But nothing remains the same forever, of course, and rather than assuming that it would stay that way, Bryce reflected long and hard on the consequences of any foreseeable shift of the central position of the Christian faith in America. (Whether this shift was the result of external attacks by secularists or internal erosions through secularization does not matter here.) What mattered was that if the Christian faith was foundational to the social cohesion of America in his time, what would happen if its influence diminished or collapsed? As Bryce reflected on this point, he admitted that he was "startled by the thought of what might befall this huge but delicate fabric of laws and commerce and social institutions were the foundation it had rested on to crumble away."[4]

Such an erosion did not appear likely at the dawn of the twentieth century, when America then, and for many decades afterwards, appeared the Western country least likely to drift from its traditional Christian moorings. Indeed, at that time the new world contrasted favorably with the old in terms of religion. Europe had begun to secularize significantly in the nineteenth century and over the next century produced some of the most secular societies in history, but America remained an anomaly—both the most modern country in the world and the most religious of modern countries. Yet it was also true that Europe, for all its apparent abandonment of the Christian faith and Christian morality, did not seem to fall victim to any loss of social cohesion. In terms of ideas, Europe was horribly vulnerable to post-Christian ideologies such as Marxism and National Socialism, but at the social level it was often held together by forces such as tradition and the social cohesion of its small towns and villages—a reality America had left behind long before.

Then what might happen, Bryce asked, if religion were to crumble away in America? That is what startled him. For "America is the country in which the loss of faith in the invisible might produce the completest revolution, because it is the country where men have been least wont to revere anything in the visible world."[5] "Completest revolution?" His insight was radical. American society was so free, so mobile and so fast and ever-changing that the only thing holding America together was religion, and if religion were to lose its inner vitality and its social influence, there would be unimaginable consequences.

Unquestionably, only a century later the "completest revolution" has taken place. Neither the Christian faith nor any other religion or ideology holds that position in America now. And today's conditions of ever-expanding diversity, now including an absurd and bewildering range of possible sexual identities, have also seen a fateful loosening of any point of genuine unity. The original American motto has been knocked off its balance, so that the *unum* has been downplayed and the *pluribus* has run riot. Americans have even squandered the genius of their traditional understanding of religious freedom and its significance for knowing how to live with the deepest differences.

W. B. Yeats's famous line, "Things fall apart; the centre cannot hold," was written in his poem "The Second Coming" in 1919, after the grand disillusionment of World War I. For the United States the collapse of the center happened in the 1960s, including the disillusioning aftermath of the Vietnam War. But America has now followed Europe, and the outcome will be equally consequential. The present state of affairs may be captured in three facts.

First, the former Jewish and Christian covenantal agreements that were the center of American life have been assaulted and have collapsed. The covenant is broken.

Second, no other set of ideas has so far succeeded in replacing these foundational beliefs, so America is presently decentered, centerless, unbonded or unglued, and in the throes of a culture war to decide which beliefs and values will be the supreme authority and point of unity in the culture.

Third, as the culture war has deepened, the rivalry to replace the former Jewish and Christian center has heated up, and in the process has damaged other parts of the American heritage. There is therefore not only no center but no civil way to establish one, for America has severely discounted its heritage of religious freedom—and its genius for making it possible for a society with diverse faiths to live with its deepest differences. All that is left is power plays.

As a result of this crisis, the political, economic, racial and cultural polarizations in America are widening and proving impossible to heal; the foundational ideas that built the American political order are losing their compelling power; highly illiberal and un-American ideas and practices are rearing their head; statesman-like leadership is conspicuous by its absence, and America's social cohesion is fraying. All that remains to be seen is the timing and direction of the consequences for the future of the American experiment.

Progressives will dismiss Bryce's observation as the gloomy forebodings of an anxious conservative. It is true that his point fits more comfortably with traditional conservative thinking. The French philosopher Joseph de Maistre, for example, famously argued that the larger and more diverse a nation was, the more likely it was that it would need to be held together and governed either by coercion or, if it desired to be free, by religion. But John Locke argued the same thing in "A Letter Concerning Toleration" in 1689: "The taking away of God, but though even in thought, dissolves all."[6] And the historians Will and Ariel Durant seconded the motion. "There is no significant example in history, before our time, of a society successfully maintaining moral life without the aid of religion."[7]

In fact Bryce was not a reactionary like de Maistre. He was an unashamed liberal, and his comments were based on his observations of the historical and social role of religion in America, just as ours should be too. The United States is facing an appalling rise in violence, but contrary to President Obama, the deepest reason is not lack of gun control but the fact that in community after community the center is not holding. There is a natural warp and woof to any fabric, just as there is to any society's moral and social ecosystem, and when that natural condition is ignored, fabrics will unravel, glacier-like solidities will melt, and societies will lose their cohesion. There is a point at which all the king's horses and all the king's men will not be able to put Humpty together again.

ALL THAT IS SOLID MELTS INTO AIR

If the first trend is relatively obvious, the second is nothing of the sort. But what is it, we must ask, that causes the mudslide effect, that triggers the erosion, the fraying, the unraveling, the melting or whatever metaphor we wish to use? The idea that there is something at work is not recent. In the first chapter of *The Communist Manifesto*, published in 1848, Karl Marx used the metaphor of "melting" in describing something he saw at work in the early industrial revolution and the rise of market capitalism:

All fixed, fast-frozen relations, with their train of ancient and venerable prejudices and opinions, are swept away, all new-formed ones become antiquated before they can ossify. All that is solid melts into air, all that is holy is profaned, and man is at last compelled to face with sober senses his real condition of life, and his relations with his kind.[8]

We are apt to miss Marx's point—to our loss. For one thing, he and his legacy have become toxic because of their horrendous totalitarian consequences. But Marx could be highly perceptive and sometimes caring, especially when he was younger, and he was certainly ahead of his times in observing how the solid was melting into air, and that this was more than a matter of ideas only. And for another thing, we are the grateful heirs of the twin shapers of our advanced modern world—the industrial revolution and market capitalism, so we are prone to forget the savage dislocations in traditional life that was the price paid by the first two generations experiencing the Industrial Revolution. We are therefore liable to view only the benefits of modernity and not to appreciate its costs.

Nietzsche has his own famous term to describe the same effect: the *death of God*. He was not the first to use the term. Hegel among others had used the term seventy-five years before him, but Nietzsche was the most radical in pressing home the consequences in every area. The death of God was far more than a crisis for theology and theologians. It was an all-encompassing catastrophe that touched the whole of culture and all the values and disciplines that had depended on God—including such important things as truth, reason, knowledge, morality, right, wrong, good, evil, art, philosophy and the humanities. Every one of them must change and be drastically revalued. God was dead, the sun had been destroyed, the cosmic order had been unhinged, the center had collapsed, and everything that had once depended on them was now hollowed out, empty, vacuous and sheer vanity. Nothing would ever be the same again. In losing God the Western world had lost its soul and its center. It had become "weightless"—groundless, centerless, meaningless, insignificant and immaterial, with an "unbearable lightness of being."[9]

Clearly, both Marx and Nietzsche were pointing to the same historic and momentous meltdown in Western civilization, but they each focused on different reasons. Nietzsche's analysis was philosophical. He focused on crisis of faith and culture that stemmed from the "murder" of God, whereas Marx's analysis was sociological. He focused on something that was happening in the rise of the modern world itself and in its effect on how people lived their lives and went about their business in the industrial age. Nietzsche's point is the more obvious today, whereas Marx's is less so and intriguing. But it still does not get to the bottom of our original question. All that is solid may be melting into air, but why?

Zygmunt Bauman, a Polish sociologist and former professor at the University of Leeds in Britain, has developed the idea of *melting* further than anyone. He has written extensively on globalization and modernity, and a recurring theme is his use of the metaphor "liquid." Keying off Marx's phrase, he describes our world in terms of its being "liquid modernity," "liquid times," "liquid life" and "liquid love."[10] Using the *Encyclopedia Britannica* definition, he points out that a solid is something that has sufficient bonding to be able to hold its atoms together and therefore to retain its shape when it is at rest, whereas a liquid or a gas cannot. Fluids are ready to change their shape at any moment according to the space they occupy. They flow, flood, spread, leak, seep, ooze and drip, and are not easy to stop—just like the mudslide.

All that is solid has melted into air, but the stage between the melting and the evaporation is liquid. In other words, we have moved from the fixed world of tradition and identity to the fluid world of modernity, where everything always changes and nothing keeps its shape for very long. There is therefore a mind-boggling variety to choose from in modern life, starting with something as basic as identity, but each one carries a sense of frailty, temporariness and vulnerability. Identity is never achieved, solid and lasting. People and things are always becoming, but they never become anything for long. They are undefined, incomplete, indeterminate and open to the new. The modern world is always under construction, and everything is provisional, for the time being, and until further notice.

No choice must be irrevocable. Choice should be noncommittal, for the worst thing is to mortgage your future by a choice that is binding and allows you no freedom to change or to move on. After all, there may be a better option tomorrow, a higher-paying job down the road, a more attractive husband, wife or partner at the next party, or a more spacious and magnificent home elsewhere, or a more appealing identity and a more fashionable sexual orientation. Keep your eyes wide open and your options open too. Give the kaleidoscope another turn and a fresh pattern of reshuffled possibilities awaits you. Tomorrow is a new day with new options. Freedom is the freedom to maneuver, and ties that bind must never become ties that bog you down.

In short, the advanced modern liquid world with its liquid life and its liquid loves is protean. It is always liable to change shape. Its only constant is change. Its only certainty is uncertainty. Liquid life is always formless, flowing, oozing, leaking and seeping—again, uncomfortably close to the mudslide effect.

What then are the causes for the meltdown and the mudslide? Why is it that solid, bedrock traditional realities such as the family and marriage appear to have melted into a hundred malleable shapes? What has happened to such assured religious beliefs as the Christian faith that they appear so weightless and insubstantial, even to some who believe them? The answer, I believe, is that at the heart of advanced modernity are a trio of factors (the three dark Rs) that have converged to form a kind of black hole that attracts, pulverizes and melts all that is solid and certain in life. The result has been called "zombie ideas" and "zombie institutions," ones that are "dead and still alive." Once again, these factors may be set out in three comments.

First, advanced modernity breeds a *radical relativizing of claims and certainties*, through which postmodernism reduces all truths to the level of undecidable.

Second, advanced modernity creates a proliferating *range of choices* through which it reduces all serious choice to the level of a noncommittal and nonbinding preference for the moment.

Third, advanced modernity produces an unprecedented *rapidity of change*, through which modern life turns "This too shall pass" into a grand liquidizer of solidities, until everything is reduced to dust, as light as air, fleeting and inconsequential.

Can Christian faith regain its spiritual, theological and cultural solidity so that it stands impervious to such trends? So that no black hole can ever swallow it? Can Christian marriages and families be restored to resemble rocks rather than sand, redwoods rather than tumbleweed? It goes without saying that the biblical counterpoint to weightlessness is *glory*, God's glory, for the root meaning of *glory* is the weightiness and solidity that comes from reality. The Greeks and the Romans believed in glory too. Indeed, they lived, strove and fought for excellence and glory in field after field. But they put their emphasis on the external aspects of glory—the renown, the reputation and the fame that radiates out from the heroic accomplishment of a victorious general, a winning athlete or a laurel-crowned playwright at a festival. But since it was external, such glory was only external and always fleeting. As the Greek poets expressed it, such glory lasted only "as long as the bard sings and the child remembers." Our own Western view of glory is much the same. We celebrate our winners, our gold medalists, our Hall of

Famers and our most valuable players, but the glory is always external and therefore fading.

The Bible's view of glory is quite different. Because of the unique character of God, who simply is and beside whom there is no other, the emphasis is on the internal, and it speaks of the weightiness, the gravitas, that comes from the ultimate reality of God being God. The Lord whom we worship is *Only*. He is *Other*. And he is *Over all*. So yes, the Lord wins great renown, through the moral excellence of his character, the power of his word and the splendor of his deeds. But his is the ultimate glory, and his glory lies far deeper than renown. It stems from the reality of his very being as God. He has glory because he is the ultimately and only "real reality" that is the ground and source of all other reality anywhere. All other reality is created reality, including each of us as human beings and the vast cosmos around us. Neither we nor the universe were self-created, and we are not self-sustaining. We are derived from God and dependent on God.

Nietzsche was therefore closer to the truth than he realized. When cultures reject God, they cut themselves off from the ultimate ground of reality, and in the end they do indeed become weightless, insubstantial, light as air, ephemeral or, in the terms used by the prophets, "weighed in the balances, and found wanting" (Dan 5:27 KJV). They give birth "*only* to wind" (Is 26:18), and like tumbleweed before the hurricanes of history, they are eventually "gone with the wind" (Is 57:13). The judgment over their end is the verdict "Ichabod"—the glory, the reality, the weightiness has gone (1 Sam 4:21).

The opposite of the weightlessness that leads to a nation's collapse is revival, a return to the glory and therefore the reality and weightiness of God. When a country as a whole, or the people of God within a country, realize their bankruptcy in turning away from the source of all reality, they can repent and turn back to God.

And their prayer then will be for revival and reformation, when the Lord will graciously fulfill his promise once again:

> For the earth will be filled
> With the knowledge of the glory of the LORD,
> As the waters cover the sea. (Hab 2:14)

When Moses found himself in the supreme crisis of his life, after the revolt of the golden calf, he prayed what is surely the most daring prayer in the Bible: "Show me Your glory" (Ex 33:18). He was asking to know all of the reality of God that a fallen human being could be allowed to see and still live. No one could ever see God fully and live, but he knew that in this direst test of his leadership, nothing less than knowing God as ultimate reality would see him through.

As we survey the poor state of the Christian church in the Western world in the advanced modern world of the early twenty-first century, our challenge and its answer is the same.

ALL ON OUR OWN, AND ALL UP TO US

The third trend is the oldest of the three—the Babel-like drive of evolutionary atheistic humanism to build a new humanity and a new world without God. In sum, a "new Empire of Man," as the Club of Rome describes it. This age-old attitude goes back almost as far as the fall, but has been given a powerful new lease of life and a momentous new opportunity by the advanced modern world. In the words of the founder of the Club of Rome, "Man, from having been one of the many creatures of the planet, has now cast over it his uncontrasted empire. . . . *The age of the empire of man looms before us.*" "This global empire possesses the wherewithal to out-shine all past civilizations." Humanity is now the "leader of life" and *"moderator of life on the planet—including his own life."*[11] "We're all on our own in the universe, and it's all up to us" is the rallying cry of this philosophy.

Needless to say, none of the three terms in "evolutionary atheistic humanism" is new. Evolution owes its ancestry to Charles Darwin; sophisticated versions of atheism go back through Latin poets such as Lucretius to Greek philosophers such as Democritus. And in its modern form, humanism has formed a strong strain of Western life ever since the Renaissance and the writings of Pico della Mirandola. But what has brought them together in a fateful new way is the combination of the stunning advances of science, especially biogenetics, and the radical forms of the philosophy of *social constructionism.*

Social constructionism is a theory that seeks to analyze the way in which we are shaped by our shared beliefs and ideas as we live together in our different societies, so that it can be said that we all take part in constructing the reality we share in our own society. In other words, reality is not given us by nature. There is no such thing as a creation order, as Christians understand it, or sacred ontology, as Jews understand it—meaning that good and evil are objective facts about the universe. Rather, if we wish to understand what we see as "reality," and it should always have quotation marks around it because it is always so-called reality; we have to trace the impact of our social context on our thinking. This insight is of course correct in part and very important as far as it goes. Obviously we all see things somewhat differently because we are shaped by our different social settings, or Pascal put it famously, "True on this side of the Pyrenees, false on the other."[12] Rightly understood, that is a key insight for Christian apologetics.

But the radical form of the philosophy goes much further and a step too far when it claims that all human knowledge is socially constructed—*and nothing more.* What we know is so shaped by our social context, they say, that any claim to be true or false, right or wrong, is not only absurd but irrelevant. What we call truth is itself only a matter of human convention or social construction. Commonly accepted truths are really social constructions that have been solidified to the point where they are now accepted as true, natural and self-evident. This conclusion is brutally destructive in two ways. For one thing, it undermines an objective view of truth because it denies that there is any final essence to anything. There is no core of objective truth or reality to anyone or anything at all. There is no "there there."

If everything we know is only socially constructed, including our view of truth and reality, that means that what we take to be reality is always humanly devised. It is manmade, a social fiction or, in the jargon of the academy, "an imagined reality." This does not mean that it is a lie, for a lie is an intention to deceive. Rather, we have all agreed to play the same game, and so long as we enjoy the game and follow the rules, we are not deliberately lying but only suspending disbelief. Such imagined realities are an unwitting fiction that everyone believes in, having forgotten where they came from and how they were constructed. As such, they will be real in their consequences so long as people keep playing the game. Anthropologist Harari's description of the shared myths of religion is typical:

> None of these things exist outside the stories that people invent and tell one another. There are no gods in the universe, no nations, no money, no human rights, and no laws and no justice outside the common imagination of human beings.[13]
>
> It is an iron rule of history that every imagined hierarchy disavows its fictional origins and claims to be natural and inevitable.[14]

Equally importantly, this radical form of the philosophy provides impetus to a radical style of political tactics. It invites an attack on all accepted truths, because unmasking the social fictions is seen as the way to liberate ourselves from the oppression of the socially constructed realities that have imprisoned us without our realizing it. In short, the term *socially constructed* is now a bugle call to arms. When radicals use it, the term is shorthand for an open invitation to an assault on tradition and on long-held ways of seeing and doing things. First, there must be a liberation from God and therefore from meaning and ethics, from solid institutions such as marriage and the family, and from all inhibiting categories such "the binary opposites" of "male" and "female." And second, there must be a liberation from nature and even from what was considered our own nature, so that we can be truly free.

As I write, the headlines are trumpeting the stories of a sixty-five-year-old male Olympic athlete who has become a forty-five-year-old woman and a six-foot-tall, fifty-two-year-old married man who has become a six-year-old girl in frilly dresses. Transgenderism will almost certainly become the phase of the sexual revolution that overreaches and becomes "a change too far." But for the moment we are becoming engulfed by the infamous pronoun wars in which *he, she* and *it* are pronounced to be identity straitjackets that imprison us within "heteronormativity." Far from being bullied into any fixed identity, we are told we are all somewhere along a spectrum and encouraged to understand ourselves as "gender fluid." ("Sometimes I feel feminine and masculine at the same time, and other times I reject the two terms entirely.") LGBTQI activists currently offer us eight different possible pronouns—including the honorific title *mx* for those who do not wish to identify themselves as either male or female.

The term *social constructionism* is new, but not the idea. In *Leviathan*, for example, Hobbes argued for just such an extreme relativism. ("There being nothing simply and absolutely so; nor any common Rule of Good and Evil, to be taken from the nature of objects themselves.")[15] Rousseau held the same view. If "man is born free, but everywhere is in chains," then our primal natural state is free, but all that is added and outside our primal state is constructed and artificial, and therefore a candidate for revolutionaries to attack as oppressive and to be torn down in the name of releasing our original freedom.

Today's most obvious example is the sexual revolution, where a key principle of Rousseau's heirs is that gender trumps biology. This means that the reality of biology and the natural order of things must be minimized, either through cultural coercion or through surgery, whereas the place of gender and socially constructed views of male and female must be highlighted in whatever direction different activists might wish to go. But of course, they say, what has been socially constructed is the prison of which we are not aware, so the various liberation movements must each deconstruct all that oppresses its victims anywhere, starting with such oppressive basic categories as male and female. Only when these categories and their like are all dismantled can the progressives then construct a revolutionary new world for each of the expanding parts of what was once simply the fourfold description of the LGBTQI movement.

Just so do our contemporary social constructionists set about dismantling marriage and the family, shifting their responsibilities to the state and the market, neither of which can or should handle them, and so triggering what bids to become one of the most disastrous social revolutions in all history.

Talk of the sexual revolution far outweighs talk of political revolution today, but the same radical dismantling could be applied to our countries' political orders too and with equally devastating effect. After all, we are told, political beliefs are not a matter of objective truth or real justice. Their principles have no objective validity. They are "shared myths," powerful through their consequences and therefore a social force—so long as they are still believed together. Of course, we all understand where that dismissive analysis leads. After all, we apply it condescendingly to earlier cultures, such as the Greeks and the Romans, with their myths of Athena and Jupiter. But the same analysis is now being applied to us in ways that are lethal to what remains of the civilization of the West.

What, for example, is the standing of such foundational statements as Magna Carta, the Declaration of Independence, the US Constitution and the Universal Declaration of Human Rights? We must not mistake them, we are told, for matters of truth and truly objective ideals, let alone Thomas Jefferson's "self-evident" truths. They are merely a "cooperation manual" for hundreds of millions of modern citizens of the United Kingdom, the United States and the world. Believing them helps us "cooperate better," for how else can large swathes of people cooperate effectively except through shared myths? Cease to believe in the shared myths, or silence other people's belief in them, and the myths will prove no more lasting than those of the ruined temples of Zeus and the fallen statues and ideologies of Marx.

At this point, the cut-flower crisis of the West should be plain with a harsh clarity that no one can miss. A natural order will always appear as natural and stable as the universe itself and almost as unshakable, but an imagined order is always a skeptic's assault away from collapse. Just translate the Declaration of Independence into terms that fit the narrative of evolutionary humanism, for example, and what happens to key terms such as *created equal, endowed, Creator, unalienable rights* and *liberty*? In Yuval Harari's translation:

> According to the science of biology, people were not "created." They have evolved. And they certainly did not evolve to be "equal." The idea of equality is inextricably intertwined with the idea of creation. The Americans got the idea of equality from Christianity, which argues that every person has a directly created soul, and that all people are equal before God.

However if we do not believe in the Christian myths about God, creation, souls, what does it mean that all people are created "equal"? Evolution is based on difference, not on equality. Every person carries a somewhat different genetic code, and is exposed from birth to different environmental influences. This leads to the development of different qualities that carry with them different chances of survival. "Created equal" should therefore be translated "evolved differently."[16]

In its concentrated and undiluted form, the philosophy of social constructionism contains a cocktail of toxic ideas that are far too easily accepted today. "It's all in the mind," the activists say. But what that means is that some alternative is in somebody's mind, so you better watch out if what is in your mind differs from what is in theirs. Three maxims in particular have grown out of it to form a salient part of the mentality of the advanced modern world. Along with the destructive components of the two previous trends in this chapter, they have become notable features of the heart of modern darkness: no givens, no rules and no limits.

First, there are *no givens* in human life (and certainly no divinely created order or even a natural moral order), so that categories such as true or false, right or wrong, male or female are relative and depend entirely on one's viewpoint. Everything, absolutely everything, is socially constructed and everything is permitted.

Second, there are *no rules* in human relationships (and certainly no Ten Commandments, Golden or Silver Rule, or natural law). Everything is socially constructed.

Third, there are *no limits* to human endeavor. Given enough time and human ingenuity, everything can be socially constructed and will be. The challenge, it is said, is not to predict the future but to invent it. (A Silicon Valley researcher said, "A million-year lifespan? If it's possible, why not?")

Quite obviously, these three maxims are a deliberate flouting of the foundational ethics of both Judaism and the Christian faith and a savage devastation of the root system of Western civilization. For both the Jewish and Christian faiths, and a key part of their strength as the working faith of the West, is the assumption that there are indeed givens. The universe has a created order, including right and wrong, true and false, male and female, and therefore it has an ethical and social ecology just as it has an environmental ecology. Respect this order and the result will be the blessing of a multilevel prosperity, but reject it and the outcome will be the curse of deepening chaos and disaster. In short, there is an ethical equivalent to the second law of thermodynamics. Like all systems and institutions, nations and civilizations lose energy over time, and the idea of ever-innovating, self-engineered perpetual growth is a mirage. Social construction is anti-Jewish, anti-Christian, anti-Western and ultimately anti-human.

Let the contest between the claims begin, openly and conclusively. Choices have consequences, and the ethical wisdom of Judaism and the Christian faith stands open to the challenge of disproof. If in the coming generation America and the West thrive under the fictional or imagined ethics of social constructionism, then Judaism and the Christian faith will be exposed as wrong. But if indeed these faiths are true, the created order is real and its ethical standards are good, then America will not flourish and the link between America's disobedience and America's degeneration will become plain to all—probably in terms of mounting violence and sexual chaos. According to the Hebrew and Christian Scriptures, personal integrity and public order are a necessity and not a luxury for those who desire to build just, free and stable human societies. To flout the will of God openly will therefore be the fast track to social and national failure for Western nations.

WHAT ODDS THE SUPERMAN?

No one listening to those who express the spirit of these constructionist maxims, or watch them at work, can miss a tension that rises sooner or later in the discussion. Is humanity capable of such a titanic task? And if humanity proves "all too human," as Nietzsche observed, and there is any acknowledgment of a flaw in human nature, how is it to be overcome? On one side are the moderate optimists. There is certainly no God, they say, so we humans are on our own in the universe, and it is all up to us. But so far, the record of history shows, we have not proved capable of transcending the destructive consequences of our innate egotism and violence.

So what we need, Aurelio Peccei says, in a flourish of religious sounding words, is a "redeeming humanism. . . . Only a New Humanism can bring about such transformation in man, raising his quality and capacity up to the level of his new responsibilities." This is the sole "road to salvation."[17] "Nothing really can be done to reverse the human predicament if we do not first understand very clearly that the only road to salvation is through what I have called the human revolution—primed by a new humanism and leading to the development of a new human quality."[18] Redeeming humanism? Road to salvation? The human revolution? A new human quality? What each term means, and how this is to be accomplished, disappears into the mist as Peccei ushers on one vague term after another to endorse the vague term before it. The leap of faith required to make this vision credible makes jumping the Grand Canyon look like a stroll in the park.

On the other side are the full-blown social constructionists, impatient with such prevarications. There are no givens, there are no rules, and there must be *no limits at all*. If they find that "biology enables, but culture forbids," then culture must stand back and allow biology and science to move forward unimpeded. Is there talk of a "technological moratorium," to allow us to take a moral breather and put our house in order before we proceed? It should be dismissed as timidity. Where did the idea of the *natural* as a barrier come from anyway? It was Jews and Christians (and also Stoics) who introduced the idea of the created as natural, and if their ideas go, the idea of natural can go too.

Is this comment intended to be read as an attack on science? On the contrary. Properly understood, science is one of God's greatest gifts to humankind, as the vibrant faith of Isaac Newton and many of the very greatest scientists powerfully attest. But science is mainly about *how* and not about *why*. It tells us more and more about the facts of the universe, but not their meaning. And as Christopher Dawson points out, the history of science is not that of a simple continuous development. "It takes a different form in every culture, Babylonian, Greek, Moslem and Christian, and until a culture has created a scientific ideal that is in harmony with its own spirit, it cannot bear scientific fruit."[19] In other words, the problem in the future will never be science itself but science within the spirit of contemporary atheism in its social constructionist, neo-Babel form, which may well produce what Churchill called "the abyss of a new Dark Age made more sinister, and perhaps more protracted, by the lights of perverted science."[20]

The driving imperatives of social constructionism are clear. If anything can be done, it will be done. And if we don't do it, somebody else will. Whatever is now possible must also be natural and therefore doable, for evolution is blind in regard to values and has no higher standard by which to judge. So any part of life can be used for any purpose at all, even if quite different from its original function—so long as it advances the purported progress of evolution and the survival of the fittest. And in the last resort, there is always the "TINA card" (there is no alternative). Progress with the imprimatur of inevitability is irresistible.

Fear made the gods, the atheists say, and fearlessness will blaze the trail to the future without God. But for those who adopt this position, even ethics may have to be shouldered aside if it gets in the way of scientific advance. With dazzling prospects in view, such as a longer human lifespan, the cure of various diseases, and the decrease and elimination of all kinds of premature death, psychologist Steven Pinker does not mince words. The greatest threat to the advance of science is ethics. "Given this potential bonanza, the primary moral goal for today's bioethics can be summarized in a single sentence. 'Get out of the way.'"[21]

Get ethics out of the way? The story of evolutionary humanism is actually a cautionary tale, even in the telling of its own scientist-kings and true believers. It starts, and periodically only continues, on the basis of sheer chance. It advances down the road, but the toll charged is the oppression and monstrous slaughter of human beings as well as the wholesale extinction of other species, and its triumphs are often based on fraud and deception rather than truth. And at its end is the specter of the potential destruction of the human race and the planet itself. Yet armed with such a tale, evolutionary humanists are again setting out for their brave new worlds as if none of the past were relevant and a better future were there for the taking.

Liberal humanists and socialist humanists have largely fallen back in the race for the future, both of them indicted for being parasitic on the Jewish and Christian faiths. But evolutionary humanists are undismayed. They may part company with their earlier liberal principles; they may be impatient with talk of ethics and moratoriums; and they may soon resume dubious and discredited earlier experiments such as eugenics; but what matters is if their eyes are now fixed on glittering prizes that were once considered unattainable and the stuff of science fiction. They are the masters of the universe, and they are out to be the masters of the future. Armed with their theory of everything, their ultimate goal is to be masters of everything.

The end of human poverty and disease? Near-perfect medicine? Bionic life? A doubled lifespan? The resurrection of the Neanderthals? Triumph over death itself? Honorable "species-cide" if we can design posthuman beings, with greater intelligence than our own, and superminds to solve the earth's problems and do better than we have? It is ironic that "intelligent design" as God's design is anathema to the evolutionary humanists, but in a fit of hubris their own goal is nothing less than to replace what they see as four billion years of aimless natural selection with a new and improved intelligent design of their own.

And at the end of everything: *Singularity*. Physicists tell us that the Big Bang was a singularity, a point at which all the laws of nature that we know did not exist. But the evolutionary humanists then transfer this notion from the beginning of time and apply it to the end of history too. "We may be fast approaching a new singularity, when all the concepts that give meaning to our world—me, you, men, women, love and hate—will become irrelevant. Anything happening beyond that point is meaningless to us."[22]

The French poet Paul Valery raised a searching question to people with such attitudes: Will the human mind be able to master the world that the human mind has created? Will we, as John von Neumann predicted, become defenseless in the face of our own emancipated technology, so that it overwhelms us like the forces of natural disasters did earlier? Will our humanly made supermachines acquire such intelligence and independence that they turn into an inhuman force relieving us of the burden of human freedom and responsibility, as Zygmunt Bauman has wondered? In rejecting religion as myth, will evolutionary humanism "risk the accusation of having slain the Minotaur only to become himself the monster at the center of the labyrinth"?[23] In his last interview, in *Der Spiegel* in 1966, philosopher Martin Heidegger surveyed the human predicament in its technological labyrinth and lamented, "Only a god can save us."[24]

Considering the wonder of the workings of the universe and the contrasting horrors of so much of human history, surely only a diehard devotee would bet on the success of humanity's designs against God's designs. Yet have no fear, the evolutionary humanists chime in, we ourselves are "on the verge of becoming a god"—"the animal that became a god" and a god "poised to acquire not only eternal youth, but also the divine abilities of creation and destruction."[25] If there were gods, Nietzsche stated candidly in *Thus Spake Zarathustra*, how could he bear not to be a god? But only after he had assaulted the heavens could he be a god on earth. Hence his battle cry, "Nothing but earth!" and his summons, "Remain faithful, I adjure you, my brothers, to the earth. Do not thrust your heads into the sands of heavenly things. . . . To sin against the earth, that is now the most monstrous crime of all."[26]

Meanwhile, in the interim before the world's last days, misgivings, laments, boasts and haunting questions are mounting, and as the new technologies advance exponentially they will reach an even higher crescendo. But the one question that finally matters is, What does God think of all this? "[What] if God wearied of mankind?" Winston Churchill asked in one of his last speeches, as he pondered the nuclear crisis.[27] The truth is that the quandary raised by the Empire of Man is now similar to the quandary raised by the Tower of Babel, and in both cases humans were, and are, aware of their predicament even before God speaks. In their vaunting pride, advanced modern humanists are competing with their ancient rivals in rebellion. They are straining every nerve and brain cell to make a name for their projects and themselves. But they are driven too by an insatiable need to succeed, for only success after success after success can allow them to avert their eyes from the strains and stresses on humanity and on the earth behind them.

And what of us as followers of Jesus? What do we do as we wait to see God's mind made clear? As so often, we find ourselves standing "in the interim," living between the Word and the Judgment, so our task is to wait and to watch, always engaging the heart of the darkness, but never falling for its dark allure.

≥ A Prayer ≤

O LORD OUR GOD, sovereign Creator of time and space, you are our rock, our refuge, and the mainstay and meaning of our lives. We give you thanks that your created order is no constriction of our humanity but the firm foundation for a good life, and your will and your ways are the sure guidelines for our highest freedom and fulfillment. Our hearts were restless until they found their rest in you, and all our homes in this passing world are merely lodgings on our journey home to you. Grant that in an age that is torn between the delusions of its own chosen freedoms and the disappointments of its broken dreams, we may hold fast always and only to you and rest in your will as the best and surest path to life. Through Jesus Christ our Lord, Amen.

QUESTIONS FOR DISCUSSION

1. Lord Acton called religion "the key to history." How has faith been critical to the history of your country? What might be the effects of its declining importance or its becoming purely private?

2. What is meant by "liquid" modern life? What examples can you give of this "melting" happening?

3. What are the consequences of seeing everything in life as socially constructed? How would you argue against such a view?

chapter five

Life with No Amen

Jürgen Habermas was often celebrated as one of the world's leading intellectuals and Europe's most important secularist thinker. In a fascinating essay in 2008, "An Awareness of What Is Missing," he described the day in April 1991 when he attended the memorial service for his friend Max Frisch in St. Peter's Church, Zurich. Frisch was a Swiss author and playwright, and also an atheist, and he had left precise instructions for the service. His partner Karin Pilliod spoke, reading out a message from the deceased, and two other friends gave reflections. But as specified, there was no minister, there was no blessing, and there was no religious rite at the burial. Above all, in Frisch's own words, the entire proceedings were to be "without an 'Amen.'"

Writing nearly twenty years later, Habermas wrote that the memorial service did not seem that unusual at the time. But as the years passed, it seemed more and more strange. "Clearly Max Frisch, an agnostic, who rejected any profession of faith, has sensed the awkwardness of non-religious burial practices and, by his choice of place, publicly declared that the enlightened modern age had failed to find a suitable replacement for a religious way of coping with the final *rite de passage* which brings life to a close."[1] Along with *alleluia*, *Amen* is one of the world's most nearly universal words, and without the implicit prayer in its "Let it be" or "So may it be, Lord," there was plainly an awareness that something in human life is missing—at least from the point of view of atheism.

Starting with this event, Habermas traced the history of thought from the Axial Age to the Modern Age and argued in his essay that while the chasm between religious thought and secular thought appeared unbridgeable, the world's religions were an "unexhausted force," which must mean that there was more reason in them than their secularist critics acknowledged. What was it that such religions tapped? he asked. What gave them their resonance? He believed it was their appeal to "solidarity" or a sense of a "moral whole"—"the idea of the kingdom of God on earth." Religion is therefore valuable. "Today religious traditions perform the function of articulating an awareness of what is lacking or absent in our lives."[2]

Earlier, in 2001, Habermas had accepted the Peace Prize in Frankfurt and delivered a brief address in response, which was notable for focusing on religion. It was the first of several speeches Habermas gave on religion over the next few years, including his contribution to a book with then Cardinal Joseph Ratzinger, later Pope Benedict XVI. This clear turn in his thinking caused widespread comment. Had Habermas seen the light? Was it a significant change of mind by a leading atheist or perhaps even an intellectual conversion? Was he abandoning his longtime secularist allies? Habermas had always been notoriously tone deaf and "unmusical" and had seemingly never shown interest in any personal faith, so why this sudden new interest in religion?

At the very least, Habermas's essay represents an extraordinary acknowledgment of a key deficiency in atheism, and his voice is not alone. But beyond that essay, his later speeches and writings demonstrate a positive appreciation of the necessity of religious voices in public life. To exclude religious voices from the public square, and by extension from other open forums, is illiberal and self-defeating for democratic societies. Clearly, both these points run entirely counter to the caustic, militant and sweeping dismissals of religion by many Western atheists. Some said that Habermas had come close to admitting that secular society cannot go it alone, and it would be easy to come to that conclusion. But at the very least, his reflections open the door to a much more constructive conversation between Christians and atheists than we have seen for a while.

Is there a legitimate place for the voices of faith in public life? And how are truly liberal atheists to help that happen when some of the noisier members of their own tribe are the chief obstacles to greater freedom for all, just as some of our fellow Christians form a blockage from our side? Can Christians and atheists talk more constructively about the important differences between our faith claims and worldviews, and how we are to negotiate the differences now that their social consequences are beginning to make such a difference for the West itself?

These may seem small points in the overall challenges of our time, but they are highly significant because of the present mutual suspicion and antagonism between atheists and Christians. Many atheists view all Christians as bigoted and reactionary faith-heads who believe in God for no reason at all and resist all progress out of willful ignorance. And many Christians view atheism and atheists solely as a mortal enemy and as the people who have brazenly hijacked the Christian heritage of the West. Some Christians therefore demonize atheists and blame them as stick-figure culprits for all that is wrong in the post-Christian world.

I will never forget the demanding experience of interviewing Madalyn Murray O'Hair as the reporter for a BBC documentary, and among other famous atheists and agnostics I have met or talked to in some depth are Bertrand Russell, Arnold Toynbee, A. J. Ayer and Christopher Hitchens. So I am under no illusions: There is no question of playing down the fundamental clash between atheism and the Jewish and Christian faiths.

First, atheism is the leading contestant and rival to the Christian faith in the bitter struggle to overthrow the Jewish and Christian faiths and become the soul of the Western world and the decisive voice in Western culture.

Second, atheism is the dominant worldview among the ruling elites in the West, especially in the universities and in the press and media.

Third, in the form of the new atheists, the atheist attacks on the Christian faith and on Christians are often vicious, merciless and relentless. (Nietzsche: "The Christian conception of God . . . is one of the most corrupt conceptions of God arrived at on earth." Dawkins: "The God of the Old Testament is arguably the most unpleasant character in all fiction . . . a misogynistic, homophobic, racist, infanticidal, genocidal, filicidal, pestilential, megalomaniacal, capriciously malevolent bully.")[3]

Fourth, in the form of the strict separationists, atheists are among those who are out to do all they can, and in a scorched earth manner, to drive all religious voices from the public square and from public life altogether. For them, religious freedom is freedom *from* religion, not for religious people.

Fifth, atheism is commonly the default philosophy of the shock troops of many of the strongest anti-Christian social movements today, such as the activists of the sexual revolution.

Sixth, when Western democracy is further corrupted, as it is inexorably, it may well be that a corrupt and illiberal liberalism will degenerate into a postliberal secular nihilism that for the world of tomorrow will be the equivalent of the dangerous ideologies of the last century.

Seventh, atheism in its modern form is not just post-Christian but ex-Christian. Along with Islam earlier and the homosexual movement more recently, atheism often displays a particular animosity toward the Christian faith and the church that is surely the bitter fruit of its directly ex-Christian origins.

Lastly, atheism in its strong forms is the supreme expression of human rebellion against God. As Christian thinkers from Origen to Dostoevsky have pointed out, atheism is the ultimate worship—of the human self in God's place. As Makar Ivanovich declares in Dostoevsky's *The Adolescent*, "It's impossible for a man to exist without bowing down; such a man couldn't bear himself, and no man could. If he rejects God, he'll bow down to an idol—a wooden one, or a golden one, or a mental one. . . . They're all idolaters, not godless, that's how they ought to be called."[4]

In sum, our eyes should be wide open, and no one should understand me as saying anything else. Progressive secularism is the driving philosophy of those who are out to join Nietzsche in murdering God and attempting to return the West to the paganism of the pre-Christian world. If that sounds extreme, think of today's much-trumpeted links to classical philosophers such as Epicurus and Lucretius, or consider such social and ethical "triumphs" of progressive secularism as sexual permissiveness, adultery, easy divorce, abortion, homosexuality and euthanasia. These were all features of the world that the Romans accepted as normal and the early church combated as wrong. Above all, consider the possible rise of what Christopher Dawson in 1935 warned of as "democratic totalitarianism."[5] It was disastrous for the medieval church to make the mistake of taking over the role of the state and confusing the City of God with the City of Man. But it would be even more disastrous for the secular world to take over the state and for both to take over the role of the church and of religion as a whole, and thus for the City of Man to take over the City of God and treat religion as a department of state. As Dawson concluded,

The Church's real enemy is not the State but the World; that is to say secular civilization considered as a closed order which shuts out God from human life and deifies its own power and wealth. At the present day this spirit of the World is stronger than ever. It is becoming fully self-conscious and threatens to absorb the State and to constitute itself as the universal order of human life—a Church-State which would be the kingdom of anti-Christ.[6]

Atheists may be small in numbers in the world as a whole, and even in much of the West, but in terms of their philosophy, their social location in society, their long-term vision and their strategies and attitudes, they are disproportionately influential. As I said in an earlier chapter, it is often said that the fourth century AD was the hinge period between paganism and the Christian faith, and that the mid-twentieth century to the mid-twenty-first is the hinge period between the Christian faith and a new paganism. As Christians, we would dispute the latter because the transition is far from complete. But it would be a tragic mistake not to engage atheists in ways that might be beneficial both for them and for the wider interests of the Christian faith and our Western societies. Three reasons stand out above others.

RESTLESS HEARTS

The chief reason to care more deeply for atheists is simple: Christian love. The philosophy of our secularist neighbors on the planet is quite inadequate, we believe, and in the end it hurts no one more than themselves, as they are forced to acknowledge more often than they care to admit. The truth is that their secularist view of the universe and of the meaning of life is too small and does not even have room enough for them. At the end of the day it pares life down too far and leaves too much out. So atheism is always constricting, and the atheists' hearts cry out for more, "something more." As Habermas's story illustrates, there is always "something missing" in the atheist worldview, and their restless hearts betray it time and time again.

That is certainly not a claim to assert in the opening round of any discussion. Indeed, many such discussions have to weather a long barrage of attacks on the Christian faith and a considerable venting of anger before hearts and minds can begin to run deep and open up more candidly. Many other concerns raised by atheists will often come first, beginning with the way their own opening salvoes boomerang back on themselves. Christians are faith-heads and their faith is entirely irrational, Richard Dawkins and others charge in this well-worn mantra. We who believe in God believe for no reason at all and we maintain our faith against all evidence. But then Dawkins is confronted with numerous examples of those who quite plainly do believe with forceful reasons, such as most of the great scientists of the past and such eminent scientists today as physicist John Polkinghorne and his arguments for a fully warranted faith. In spite of this incontrovertible evidence, Dawkins continues to repeat the same charge blindly, regardless of the facts, even though he now knows that his charge is false and contradicted by the evidence—in a word, his claim is irrational.

Or again, Christians are inherently intolerant, atheists charge, and our iron rigidity is said to stem from our belief in monotheism and its fundamentals, absolutes and exclusiveness. To be sure, it was egregiously wrong for the late medieval church to claim that "error has no rights" and then to coerce or kill people in the name of what was claimed to be their higher good. Long before that, it was the early Christians who introduced the notion of religious liberty. A free God created free people and wished them to trust and worship him freely. The medieval church certainly sinned egregiously, but the church has confessed that sin long ago, and where have we heard such claims in the last hundred years, and who is it that echoes that monstrous claim today? It has been the atheist regimes, such as communism, that have oppressed dissent under that banner, and it is none other than the contemporary American atheist Sam Harris who writes even now, "Some beliefs are so dangerous that it may be ethical to kill people for believing them."[7]

At a far deeper level than such skirmishes, secularists themselves are the ones who are raising the most profound questions about secularism, though not yet to the length of abandoning the secularist worldview. The following are but a few examples.

What does it mean that the meaning of a system will always lie outside the system itself, and that life points beyond itself for its meaning? (Ludwig Wittgenstein: "The sense of the world must lie outside the world" and "We feel that even when *all possible* scientific questions have been answered, the problems of life remain completely untouched.")[8]

Why is it that some secularist philosophers are challenging their own secular orthodoxy? (Thomas Nagel in *Mind and Cosmos*: The current scientific orthodoxy of neo-Darwinism is "almost certainly false.")[9]

What does it say for secularism that so many of its philosophers openly admit that they *willed* to disbelieve in God? (Nietzsche: "What is now decisive against Christianity is our taste, no longer our reasons."[10] Bernard Williams: The "transcendent impulse" that has persisted down the centuries "must be resisted." Thomas Nagel: "I hope there is no God! I don't want there to be a God. I don't want the universe to be like that." When the Austrian logician Kurt Gödel devised what he thought was an unanswerable version of the cosmological argument for God, he told his friends that he was not about to believe his own conclusions.)[11]

Why is it that, contrary to what people think, we can learn more about humanity from history than from science? (As John Lukacs notes, history seeks to understand human beings as agents and subjects, whereas in science they can never be more than objects.)

How do secularists hope to help the advanced modern world rise above a hedonistic mass culture and civilization when they have no strong values to offer, let alone transcendent values, when they have deliberately destroyed such institutions as tradition and the family, and when they are now intent on gutting the independence of the world of civil society and allowing it to be invaded by the forces of the state and the market?

And for Christians there is always an added question to ponder: Why is it that so many of the deepest and most brilliant converts to the Christian faith, such as W. H. Auden, C. S. Lewis, Alexander Solzhenitsyn and Francis Collins, have all converted decisively from atheism?

The weight of such questions underscores Habermas's earlier point, which historian Peter Watson describes as the heart of "the modern secular predicament." For all the secularist claims down the centuries, some defiant and some assured, there is still an "awkwardness" (Habermas), an "unsufficiency" (Nagel) and a lack of "numinous" (Dworkin) about secularism. The truth is, Watson says, that "secularization is *still* not fitting the bill, is still seriously lacking in . . . something."[12]

Critics have long puzzled over the recurring fact that national liberation movements led by secularists have repeatedly been engulfed by religious counterrevolutions—such as secular Zionism by ultra-orthodoxy in Israel, or Nehru-style secular democracy by Hindu nationalism in India, and the national liberation front in Algeria by Islamism. Michael Walzer describes the trend as "a recurrent and, to my mind, disturbing pattern," but concludes that "this unexpected outcome is a central feature of the paradox of national liberation."[13]

An obvious question is, what does this trend say of secularism? But others see an even more telling sign of this "missing something" in the recent surge of what many people would consider a massive contradiction in terms: atheist religion. No one can have missed the rash of recent books opening the subject—Ronald Dworkin's *Religion Without God*, Alain de Boton's *Religion for Atheists*, Sam Harris's *Waking Up: A Guide to Spirituality Without Religion*, and more. Even the New York Times has written of the boom of "religious nones" now attending divinity schools such as Harvard and Chicago. (With *Jane Eyre* and Harry Potter taken as sacred texts, "they get Alice-in-Wonderland lost in theology. It made me happy," one student said.) Yes, the phenomenon can be explained as part of the search for meaning and for moral language that cannot be found in the other disciplines. Yes, it can be seen as part of the general syncretism of the day—more than a quarter of American atheists think of themselves as "spiritual people," and more than a tenth even believe in God or a "universal spirit." Yes, there is an element too of copycat phenomenon ("Why should the good Lord have all the feel-good self-expression and sense of community?"), and to the extent that all these books are that, they will only be a fleeting trend that is no more significant than a publishing flavor of the month.

It would be a mistake, too, to give too much credence to many of the more trivial examples of atheistic religion, such as secularist "churches." They are unlikely to be around in twenty years time. The grand political religions of the last century cannot be dismissed so easily, but surely there is a deeper point behind the religious impulse among secularists—religion is close to ineradicable in human nature, and strict secularism is finally unsatisfying for most people and sometimes even for secularists themselves. Religion for atheists actually goes back a long way—the French Revolution's enthronement of the goddess of reason, for example, and Auguste Comte's meticulously devised but chronically unsatisfying Religion of Humanity, in which the French Revolution replaced the incarnation and the calendar was restarted in 1789. Hailed by its founder as the "true religion" and the "final religion," it proved to have little popular appeal and no staying power. To the recurring dismay of secularists, "secular religion" has always proved to be both deeply needed and yet a thin, tasteless and unsatisfying gruel when it is served up.

It is notable, too, how people resort to religious language when they are stretching to make a point they can make no other way, even at the cost of sounding absurd. (Actor Jamie Foxx at the Soul Train Music Awards in 2012: "Give an honor to God and our lord and savior Barack Obama." Or Louis Farrakhan: "You are the instruments that God is going to use to bring about universal change, and that is why Barack has captured the youth. And he has involved young people in a political process that they didn't care anything about. That's a sign. When the Messiah speaks, the youth will hear, and the Messiah is absolutely speaking.")[14]

But the truth is that at a deeper level still two other forces are in play. First, at the public level, atheists often admit a need for religion in order to rule or to maintain public order. Voltaire stated it most famously in the *Letter to the Author of the Three Impostors*: "If God did not exist, one would have to invent him. I want my attorney, my tailor, my servants, even my wife to believe in God, and I think I shall then be robbed and cuckolded less often." But Machiavelli stressed the same point earlier for his prince, and the outcome is common in many atheist regimes—the state seeks to domesticate religion as its department of state.

And second, at the personal level, atheists often need some sense of religion to assuage the longing for "something more." They repeatedly betray the sense that there is something missing in their lives. Again and again, atheists let slip a lingering nostalgia for a lost world. Henry Sidgwick, professor of moral philosophy at Cambridge in the nineteenth century, was typical of many in his generation when it was said of him that while his mind rejected any faith, his heart yearned for one.[15] The poet Rainer Maria Rilke was similarly said to be "a melancholy atheist, a non-believer with a guilty conscience."[16] Playwright Peter Shaffer put the point bluntly in *Equus*: "Without worship you shrink. It's as brutal as that."[17] Philosopher Iris Murdoch expressed it more wistfully when she asked, "But is there something where God used to be?"[18]

Nietzsche summarily dismissed such thoughts as nostalgia and a chasing after shadows. "God is dead: but given the way of men, there may still be caves for thousands of years in which his shadow will be shown. And we—we still have to vanquish his shadow."[19] But it is undeniable that his own last thoughts were so dark and so far from the triumphant hymns of Zarathustra that he has been described as a man stoned by his own hand. "I will not hide it from you. Things are going very badly," he wrote to his friend Franz Overbeck. "Night overwhelms me more and more. It is as if there had just been a flash of lightning. One moment, I find myself plunged into my element, into my light. And now it is passed. I believe I am walking ineluctably to my ruin. . . . The barrel of a gun is now a source of relatively pleasant reflections for me. . . . everything is so destitute of sense."[20]

The hard truth is that life with no *Amen* is smaller, colder, darker and less welcoming for the human heart. The world of the atheists is deaf to their own aspirations, and they are homeless in the lonely world that is all that they know of home. Only the brave and the few can stand such a bleak and orphaned horizon. Secularists will simply have to face the fact that religion is here to stay, so unless their atheism is imposed coercively, as it was under totalitarian communist regimes, it will always be a minority belief. The French philosopher Ernest Renan held that "religion is necessary. The day when it disappears the very heart of humanity will dry up."[21] Emile Durkheim was no less emphatic: "There is something eternal about religion."[22] Christopher Lasch drove the point home tersely: "There is no substitute for religion. Religion is the substitute for religion."[23]

THE ILLEGITIMATE CHILD OF THE CHURCH

A second reason to reach out to atheists is that we as Christians are more responsible for atheism in the West than we often realize and acknowledge. It is easy to trace the story of atheism back to the Greeks and the Romans, and so to follow it from Epicurus and Democritus to Lucretius, Machiavelli, Montaigne, Denis Diderot, Baron d'Holbach, David Hume, Ludwig Feuerbach, Friedrich Nietzsche and all their modern heirs right down to "Ditchkins," Terry Eagleton's famous amalgamation of Richard Dawkins and Christopher Hitchens. But such a list is often left as lifeless as reading a biblical genealogy of who begat whom, who begat whom, who begat whom, ad infinitum. But of course the biblical genealogy itself is far from a dry list of names. It is packed with people whose real lives were a riotous explosion of heroism, crimes, adulteries and follies that are rich and fascinating.

So it is with the story of atheism. Atheism has its heroes, hypocrites and blackguards too, but any honest account has to acknowledge the sorry role of the church in fueling the rejection of the faith and stoking the force of atheism. This is sadly plain in the case of European atheism. There is no question that there is a direct link between the intensity of the convictions of atheism and the intolerance of the European church's attitude to dissent. The late Renaissance period was the golden age of dissimulation because it was too dangerous to think freely in public. People who did not agree with the Catholic Church did not say what they thought. Often they said the opposite of what they thought, and sympathetic readers learned to read what the authors wrote as if it were in code. Nothing was quite what was being said.

"Dissimulation is one of the most notable qualities of this age," Montaigne wrote in the sixteenth century.[24] A little later Descartes wrote that he did not wish to suffer the same fate as Galileo, so he would abide by the maxim of the Roman poet Ovid, "He has lived well, who has remained well hidden."[25] Earlier, Cesare Cremonini, an Italian Aristotelian, admitted that he did not have a shred of piety, but he wished to be thought pious. His maxim captured the dissimulation perfectly: "Within, as you please; out of doors, as custom dictates."[26] Today, we object rightly to the stifling political correctness of many campuses and parts of public life in the West, but we have to confess with sorrow that the church's earlier intolerance was political correctness writ large, and behind it were the threat of its sanctions—the gallows and the stake. It is a tragedy of historic proportions that God made the mind free, but the church made it necessary for people who wished to think freely to reject the faith and call themselves freethinkers in contrast.

In the eighteenth century the same sad situation lies behind one of the distinctive differences between the French and the American revolutions. Religion in France was oppressive, and the French Revolution was antireligious, whereas faith and freedom fought side by side on behalf of the American Revolution. Voltaire was a deist rather than an atheist, but his famous signing off at the end of his letters, "Crush the infamous thing!" (*Ecrasez l'infame*) clearly demonstrated the problem that church had become and the direction the French revolution would go.

It is true that, prior to the monstrous evils of Russian, Chinese and Cambodian communism, the French Revolution's Reign of Terror and its suppression of the uprising in the Vendée are two of the blackest marks against the history of secularist regimes. But the church's role in the background to the revolution is equally a black mark against the Christian faith. Diderot's maxim, trumpeted later by the Jacobin radicals, expressed the oppressive situation aptly. The French would never be free "until the last king had been strangled with the guts of the last priest." The church and the state, or "throne and altar," were in close collusion, and both were oppressive, so the revolution set out to throw off both. From then on, freedom and atheism have been linked fatefully in the DNA of the French people. Europe has long been the most aggressively secular continent in the world—for example, the 1920s foundation of the League of Militant Atheists—but the tragedy is that the main reason for Europe's secularity is its reaction to the corrupt and oppressive state churches in the past. In Nietzsche's words, Christian ethics had become "a capital crime against life."[27]

If this point is true of grand political events such as the French Revolution, it is also true in the lives of countless individual atheists. Benedict Spinoza, for example, was a descendant of the Marranos, Spanish Jews who were subjected to forced conversion by Spain but continued to practice their faith in secret. Bertrand Russell lost his mother when he was two and his father before he was four. He was brought up by his staunchly Victorian Christian grandmother, who gave him no freedom to think and had a habit of answering his questions by shutting him up. ("What is mind?" "Doesn't matter."/ "What is matter?" "Never mind.") Not rebelling openly like his older brother Frank, Russell kept his thinking to himself, idolized the poet Shelley as his model for rebellion, declared himself an atheist when he was eighteen, and went on to make his mark as one of the most uncompromising atheists of the twentieth century. ("I think all the great religions of the world—Buddhism, Hinduism, Christianity, Islam and Communism—both untrue and harmful.")[28]

Spinoza and Russell, needless to say, were both precocious. They possessed brilliant minds and distinguished themselves in both philosophy and mathematics. But the same story has played out endlessly with different variations. Only the Lord knows how the appalling Christian treatment of his people, the Jews, has helped to produce such enemies of the church as Spinoza, Marx and Freud, but the story goes on. Not long ago I encountered an angry atheist who had been brought up in the American South. His father had been a deacon at their local church, but he had abused his mother cruelly, and the son's anger at God was the direct fruit of the father's evil and hypocrisy. Philosophy and biography are sometimes hard to distinguish, and many an atheist has a Christian past with a chip on the shoulder where a childhood blow hurt deeply and never healed.

This means that, for better or worse, the Western church is uniquely entangled with atheism. When Alexander the Great asked Diogenes the Cynic what he might do for him, the crusty old philosopher answered famously, "Stand out of my sunlight." Doubtless there were once atheists who were simply happy to disbelieve and to be left alone in their own worlds. But that is not the character of Western atheism, nor a feature of its export varieties such as Russian and Chinese Marxism. (Lenin: "Every religious idea, every idea of God, even flirting with the idea of God, is unutterable vileness.")[29] Western atheism is aggressive, universalistic, dogmatic and imperialistic, and Christians must shoulder a partial responsibility for making it so. Emil Brunner puts the point bluntly: "Thus, the de-Christianization characteristic of the modern age is, to a large extent, the product of the infidelity of the Christians to their own faith."[30] The old maxim is true, that "the worst corruption is the corruption of the best," but that does not change the result: such atheism, along with radical Islam, is the implacable foe of the church at the present moment, and we have helped to make it so.

To be sure, we must answer the atheist charges and accusations robustly, and it is certainly not hard to find example after example of atheists crying out into the darkness because of the forlornness of their conclusions. Nietzsche, Bertrand Russell, August Strindberg, Jean-Paul Sartre, Albert Camus, Ingmar Bergman, Samuel Becket—they all made statements at one time or another that seem to call into question any hope of atheism being a satisfying answer for humanity.

Again and again the bleakness of atheism becomes undeniable, and the atheists' candor in owning up to the strategies they use to escape is admirable, if forbidding—from David Hume's resort to backgammon with his friends when his philosophy left him depressed, to Bertrand Russell's admission that he read two novels a week to take his mind off the devastating thought of a nuclear holocaust, to Nietzsche's espousal of the idea of eternal recurrence:

> What, if some day or night a demon were to steal after you into your loneliest loneliness and say to you: "This life as you now live it and have lived it, you will have to live once more and innumerable times more; and there will be nothing new in it, but every pain and every joy and every thought and sigh and everything unutterably small or great in your life will have to return to you, all in the same succession and sequence. . . . The eternal hourglass of existence is turned upside down again and again, and you with it, speck of dust!"[31]

Yet we must never forget the other side of the coin, which may be expressed in the following three ironies.

First, there is a Catholic irony to the present state of atheism. It was the first, greatest and most consistent Christian attempt at building a Christian society in history—Christendom—that, because of its failures, perpetrated the worst evils upon the world, such as the Inquisition and the forced baptism of the Jews, and produced the most militantly anti-Christian reactions in history, as in the titanic earthquake of 1789 and its revolutionary tremors across the world and down through history. Think of the film *Spotlight* and the revulsion against the Catholic diocese of Boston, or worse still, think of the revulsion against the entire Catholic church in Ireland today for the same reason—sexual abuse by priests representing God and the church.

Behind this comment is a sad but inescapable fact. The alliance between the Roman Catholic Church and the Roman Empire was a key factor in the triumph of the church in the fourth century and the later rise of Christendom. But that alliance was a poisoned chalice. It meant that from the very beginning the power of Western Christendom was based on hierarchical power in the Roman style, with the pope substituting for Caesar, rather than on the covenantal style of biblical and Jewish politics. Indeed with the general run of its popes, cardinals and bishops, and with only rare exceptions such as St. Francis and the early monasteries, the Catholic Church is still wedded to its love of hierarchy. Yet it was this hierarchical power that was corrupted in the Middle Ages to produce great evils. And it has been reliance on that power that meant that Catholicism has never done justice to the biblical and Jewish understanding of covenant, and with it the very different view of the dignity of the individual person, the liberty and equality of all citizens, and the importance of curbing all power, including the power of the church.

Second, there is also a Protestant irony. It was the most zealous and spiritually powerful reformation in Christian history—the Reformation—that has produced the most thoroughgoing secular societies the world has ever seen (Britain, Germany, Netherlands, Sweden and Denmark, for a start). If the post-Catholic nations often did not want God because of their volcanic reactions to corrupt and oppressive established churches, the post-Protestant nations simply did not need God. They led the advance of modernity and produced a world that left less room for God and his people than ever considered wise and possible in history before.

Last, there is an overall Christian irony. It is a stunning truth that all too often the strongest arguments for atheism are Christians and the Christian church. Read, for example, Christopher Hitchens's *The Portable Atheist: Essential Readings for the Nonbeliever.* Much of the book is frankly tedious and often cold—no more appealing than a flat glass of champagne. But again and again the book crackles back into life when a particular writer attacks Christians and the church and works out his or her grievances. The sad truth we must bear on our hearts is that we who follow Jesus are often the leading argument for the rejection of our Lord. As the eminent Catholic historian Christopher Dawson remarks tartly, "The convinced secularists were an infinitesimal minority of the European population, but they had no need to be strong since the Christians did their work for them."[32]

UNLIKELY PARTNERS

The third reason to reach out to atheists is that Christians and atheists are indispensable to forging a constructive way forward for humanity. The simple but unavoidable point has still not sunk in for most people: one of the major problems in the modern world is how we are to live with our deepest differences when those differences are religious and ideological, and especially when those differences erupt in public life. Many people are simply too close to the problem, and caught up in it themselves, to be able recognize it as a problem to be tackled. View the problem in the form of terrorism, and the issue becomes urgent and is well covered as a security issue. But it is much more than that too. At a higher level, living with our deepest differences is a matter of the right and just ordering of our societies, and at the highest level of all, the issue is how to ensure the maximum freedom for people of all faiths.

Here, Christians as well as atheists must face an inescapable fact that lifts the present argument out of a simple culture wars format of *either* the Jewish and Christian faiths *or* secularism. A central feature of the global world is pluralization ("everyone is now everywhere"), which means simply that there can be no simple return to the former Christian consensus at the heart of the West and no simple way forward to any secularist hegemony. Both visions fail to do justice to pluralization and diversity, but this means in turn that Christians and atheists are both essential to the way forward for the Western world. They represent the two leading voices in the present debates and the two positions that now perpetuate the culture warring over religion and public life: the Christian *restorers*, who appear to wish to restore the previous consensus that favored the Jewish and Christian faiths, versus the secularist *removers*, who wish to solve the problems of religion and public life by removing religion altogether.

Pressed consistently, neither of these two views faces up to the scale of modern diversity, and neither allows for the justice and freedom of people of all faiths and none. So they both fail for the same reason, though in different ways—Christians too often fail to argue for the common good, the good of all ("Just us" rather than "justice"), and atheists too often fail to recognize that the vast majority of humankind are deeply religious, and these believers have rights too. Thus neither the "sacred public square" of one side nor the "naked public square" of the other provides the way forward to a just and free world for everyone.

How might Christians and atheists become partners in standing for a better way forward in public life, first in the West and then eventually in other parts of the world? Such a partnership might seem unlikely, but no other combination of partners would have the same chance of breaking the stalemate in the culture wars and demonstrating an open horizon for new opportunities and solutions. And surely the time is ripe for just such a partnership, for what is at stake is no less than the viability of free and open societies that are made up of extremely diverse peoples. Can such societies flourish and endure, or will today's freedom and diversity undermine each other to the fatal weakening of the societies that promote them? The stakes are extremely high, for if free and open societies fail, the turning of the political wheel can only lead backwards from corrupted democracy to new forms of tyranny or oligarchy.

Let no one misunderstand or distort what I am saying. Given their starkly different worldviews, Christians and secularists disagree, they should disagree, and they will always disagree over their religious, philosophical and ethical differences—and therefore over political and social policies. But that said, the question is, Can Christians and atheists still be cobelligerents, united in their common commitment to freedom, freedom of conscience, and the vision of justice and freedom for all in the public square—and in a manner that provides legitimacy and stability to their societies? At least three major issues must be settled if any conversation is gong to be fruitful. The first two, which I have written on extensively elsewhere, would once have been uncontroversial, but not today.[33] The third one, however, needs far wider discussion.

The first issue is the prime importance of religious freedom, or freedom of conscience, for people of all faiths—bar none. Once understood as the "first freedom," and essential to America's grand experiment in freedom, this right has been neglected, politicized and dismissed, so that it now holds a very precarious place in the essential foundations of Western freedom. Yet without it, and it is progressives who are dismissing it as political and partisan, self-professed liberals will never be other than illiberal, and there will be no chance of justice and freedom for all, and no chance either of the possibility of living peacefully with our deepest differences.

The second issue is the equally important question of the separation of church and state. Like freedom of conscience, the principle of the separation of church and state, or of religion and political power, does not come from Thomas Jefferson or the Enlightenment, as so often claimed. Nor did it, nor should it, mean that religion(s) is strictly excluded from public life. The separation of church and state is a Jewish and Christian contribution to world history, which originally came from the understanding of the uniqueness of God in relation to the gods and all that is not God. It was then marked by different milestones in history, such as the story of the Hebrew prophet Samuel, the teaching of Jesus about

God and Caesar, the letter of Pope Gelasius to the Byzantine emperor Anastasius in AD 494, ("Two there are, august Emperor, by which this world is chiefly ruled"), and the bold declarations of Roger Williams in the seventeenth century—all these precedents long before Thomas Jefferson's use of the term.[34]

The history and the purpose of the principle are vital, for without it a double corruption quickly becomes oppressive. Unless the principle of separation is respected, the church (or religion) will be corrupted when it takes over the power of the state (or political power), and the state (or political power) will be equally corrupted when the church (or religious power) becomes a political prize for power seekers to use. This corruption is clear in the theories of Machiavelli and Hobbes and in the statecraft of England's Henry VIII and France's Cardinal Richelieu, who all sought to use religion as a tool of the state to control the masses. But it is equally clear in the corruptions of late medieval Christendom, when popes and priests sought to use the power of the state as an arm of the kingdom of God. In other words, when the principle of the separation of church and state is rightly balanced, it is to the mutual advantage of both atheists and Christians, for the loser is oppression and the winners are freedom and justice.

The third issue is the notion of a modern, pluralistic secular (but neither a secularist nor a strictly neutral) state. Allow me to put forward, again, seven considerations that would encourage such a vision to proceed.[35] They are not an argument for an improper *secularist* state, which establishes or favors believers in a secularist worldview, but for a proper *secular* (this worldly) state, which protects the foundational freedom of all believers, whether religious or secularist.

First, modern secular societies depend on the ultimate solidarity of their citizens. The greater the liberty such societies enjoy and the wider the diversity they contain, the more important is the question of their unity, or the social bond, that holds them together. It is a special challenge to sustain a stable and united society under the conditions of modern liberty and diversity. To be both positive and strong, this solidarity must be built on more than law and technology.

Second, modern liberal secular societies depend on normative assumptions that they themselves cannot generate or guarantee. Reason cannot justify itself by reason alone, and in the same way a truly neutral state cannot justify itself by purely neutral values. Both reason and the liberal state must therefore become aware of their own limitations and realize that they have to look to sources outside themselves for their moral foundations.

Third, modern liberal secular societies have themselves risen from and still depend on philosophical and ethical traditions that come from outside themselves. As a matter of simple, historical record, most of these indispensable foundations of the sanctity of life, the dignity of the person, freedom, justice, equality and virtue are pre-political and religious in character. The secular state therefore depends on more than the secular.

Fourth, naturalistic or secularist worldviews are traditions limited to certain classes and social locations just as different religious worldviews are. Like all others, such worldviews are simply one set of core beliefs and worldviews among many. They have the right to every right, but no right to be privileged above any others, and no more right to be universalized today than religious views were in the past. In particular, the liberal secular state has no right to privilege secularist beliefs.

Fifth, modern liberal secular societies in the West should be viewed as postsecularist just as much as post-Christian. The Christian consensus of the European and early American past has gone, but the myth of the purely and strictly secularist state has been shown up starkly too. The modern state is a multifaith state in the sense that religious diversity is a social fact. It is therefore in the interests of the liberal state to pay due attention to the full range of the voices of its citizens and of the sources and norms of its solidarity. Religious believers of all kinds make important claims to truth as well as important contributions to society, so their rights should be respected and their voices heard if the nation is truly to be open, free, liberal and democratic.

Sixth, history contains examples of the dark pathology of secularism as well as religion, and proponents of each should acknowledge these pathologies with candor and humility. Both have brought blessings and both have brought curses to the history of civilization, and the balance sheet of each should be totted up accurately and fairly.

Seventh, the relationship of religious and secularist believers is critical to the future of modern liberal secular societies, especially as they relate in public life. If their antagonism is not to prove the undoing of liberal democracy, they must come together in the common cause of freedom, justice and humanity. Nothing is more urgent for democratic societies than the forging of a civil and cosmopolitan public square that does justice to the interests of both partners in the relationship.

Such a vision, including the notion of a civil public square with religious freedom and the separation of church and state at its heart, is literally *u-topian*—it exists nowhere at the present moment. But it is not beyond our reach, and it is surely the only way forward from the incessant culture wars over religion and public life. Some would dismiss it as idealistic, but that has always been the accusation leveled against freedom, and even idealism becomes realism when the alternative is sufficiently dire. Make no mistake: short of such a vision, there is only the disastrous prospect of endless culture warring until one extreme or the other prevails at the expense of freedom for the good of all. Down that way lies the sorry end of

Western civilization and its guardianship of some of the deepest human hopes of justice and freedom.

Can we achieve a better way? Were such principles to be agreed between Christians and secularists, or at least accepted as talking points on an agreed agenda, we might begin a good conversation without suspicion and without rancor. Eventually a fruitful partnership might emerge. Certainly it would take leadership and courage from both sides to break out of the culture warring, but only such a costly leadership would have a chance of calling each side to lay down its arms and join forces to offer the world a way forward. The alternative is stark, best captured in Aesop's parable of the frog and the scorpion. Asked to ferry a scorpion across the river on its back, the frog at first refuses, but then agrees to do so as long as the scorpion promises not to sting him. Halfway across, however, the frog feels the sting he had feared all along, and as he feels the death paralysis spreading over him, he simply asks, "Why?"

"Because that's the way I am," the scorpion replies.

There is too much anger and suspicion in play on both sides at the moment, but secularists must speak for themselves as to what they claim is their true nature and their real vision, just as Christians must too. Do secularists agree with Habermas, for example, that to exclude religious voices from the public square is illiberal? There is no question that Jesus, in Machiavelli's words, was the "unarmed prophet," and Christians who seek to advance his kingdom as he did should have no poison in their armory. Besides, in the militant aggression of the atheism we sometimes face, we Christians can recognize our own individual rebellion against God before we were each found out by grace. And we can also hear in the atheists' anger the element of justice that cries out against the sins and errors of the church that is us in previous generations. Do we differ with atheism any less because of the sins of our own Christian past? Not one bit. After genuine confession and reform, the real differences still stand,

and they must not be fudged. But the atheists are our neighbors whom we are to love, and the gospel is never more glorious than its sufficiency in speaking to the "something more" that is missing in their atheism. So our differences with atheists must be fought out firmly and unflinchingly, but with a sorrow, a humility and a grace that allows us to fight for the good of the atheists themselves, and to fight alongside them for the good of our common human future. Whether both sides can declare a truce in the midst of their centuries-long conflicts and work together for the good of humanity is an open question. It is also a vital key to the future of humanity.

≳ A Prayer ≲

O LORD, BEFORE WHOM all human hearts are open, you know the secret desires of the rebel, just as you know the longing of the seeker and the bitterness of the heart that has been wounded. You knew our wayward hearts before you rescued us by your grace. Forgive us for the inadequacy and the hypocrisy of our witness to you. Forgive us your followers for our lack of love or truth or joy, and the way we have portrayed you in ways that were false and pinched. Have mercy on all whom we have hurt by our words and put off by our actions, and all whose unbelief has been reinforced and hardened by us your followers. Grant us such an outpouring of your Spirit and your renewing love that we may make amends, and through our grateful lives and humble words may see a massive return to you by skeptics in our time. Through Jesus Christ our Lord, Amen.

QUESTIONS FOR DISCUSSION

1. How do you think and talk about atheists in general, and how would you describe your relationship to atheists you know? Some people just accept them as they are without ever raising questions about their atheism, while others tend to argue with their atheism without ever knowing them as people with a story. What would be a better way?

2. Why do atheists so often betray the longing that there must be "something more" to life? How would you answer them?

3. What would be your proposal for a vision of public life that addressed modern diversity, including the growing number of atheists?

chapter six

Yesterday, Today, Forever

F aster, Higher, Stronger" (Citius, Altius, Fortius)—The motto of the Olympic Games says it all. They are held to provide the opportunity for the world's greatest athletes to excel in their sport, to compete with each other and to seek to surpass their peers and all who competed before them, and so to grasp the laurel crown that is the nearest the world can offer to lasting fame and glory. The Beijing Olympics in 2008 were the first Chinese Olympics and a prize for the Chinese even before the first crack of the starter's gun. There were many other firsts in the first Chinese Olympics, but one of the oddest was the lack of any American runner on the podium after the relay races.

Relay running was first introduced into the Olympics in 1928, and Team USA had been on the podium at every Olympics since then, usually awarded the gold medal. But there were none at all in Beijing. Outside Jamaica, most of the fastest runners in the world that year were American, but most unusually they had no medalist in either the men's or the women's 4x100 meters relay. Why? Again and again the spectators in Beijing and around the world heard the eerie sound of a hollow aluminum tube hitting the track. The American runners had dropped the baton. The US teams had the speed and the strength, but not the art of the handoff. They were brilliant individual runners, but swift though they were, they were not a relay team.

The American malady at the Beijing Olympics is a parable of a far deeper problem affecting the advanced modern world—the problem of *generationalism* that is affecting the relationship between generations and thus affecting the modern view of tradition, or handing on the best of the memory and the practices of the past. Generationalism is the term for the distorted understanding and use of the idea of generation that is beginning to have a profound impact on advanced modern societies.

Originally, the term *generation* was rooted mostly in biology. Deriving from the Latin word *generare*, it referred to procreation, the act of producing offspring—for example, the famous biblical repetition of "begat." A generation was therefore the time it took for parents to be succeeded by children who had children in their turn. Herodotus describes a generation as thirty-three years, give or take a few years at either end. That meant that there were roughly three or four generations in each century and—importantly—that all those living at the same time were usually seen as the same generation. In Luke 11, Jesus refers six times to "this generation," and he surely meant all those of any age who were his contemporaries, whether young or old (Lk 11:29, 30, 31, 32, 50, 51).

Our more modern understanding of generation grew out of the Enlightenment and put an emphasis on culture as much as biology. It was therefore, as so often in this period, the product of German studies (philosophers such as Immanuel Kant) and French streets (the French revolutionaries). The Enlightenment put a new stress on the possibility of social change as deliberate progress, including the ideal of complete political change through revolution and on youth as the chosen catalyst for change. This was the era of Young Germany, Young Italy and later the Young Turks. Importantly too, as youth was elevated, parents and elders were discounted and then discarded as outmoded and redundant as authorities in life.

Generations had always included some acknowledgment of culture, as opposed to biology, but it was usually rather broad—the classical era or the Augustan, Elizabethan or Georgian eras. But as the world modernized and change speeded up, the term increasingly referred to age cohorts shaped by the same cultural experiences. Dating became destiny. In the US in the twentieth century, for example, the Lost Generation (of the First World War) was followed by the Greatest Generation (the Second World War), and then in turn by the Silent Generation (postwar), the Baby Boomers (1946–1964), Generation X (1965–1980), Generation Y or the Millennials (1981–) and so on.

As this narrowing of the generations proceeded apace, some features of the new usage became clear. The emphasis was always on the distinctive features of each generation and therefore the strong differences between them. There was little self-awareness of how the term *generation* was being put to use. And there was almost no discussion of consequences of the new usage and therefore of the stakes for society. Of the features of the new emphasis, the following have become the most important.

First, generation became a key way of describing identity. ("I'm a child of the sixties," "He's a boomer," "She's a millennial.")

Second, generation became a new form of relativism, added to such other categories as class, race, gender and religion. ("It's a generational thing. You wouldn't understand.")

Third, generation became a reinforcement of the crisis of authority. ("Don't trust anyone over thirty!" and "Question authority.")

Fourth, generationalism helps to undermine wider and longer frames of responsibility and solidarity and therefore puts no checks on such problems as deficit spending (generational theft), environmental degradation (generational irresponsibility), abortion (generational murder), the social security crisis (generational wars) and the careless extinction of other species. ("What has the future ever done for us?") Dostoevsky warned of this long ago: "Why should I love my neighbor or posterity, which I shall never see, which will know nothing about me, and which in turn will disappear without leaving any traces or memories?"[1]

Fifth, generationalism aggravates the breakdown of sustainability and of living tradition. Instead of tradition being honored as a matter of *safe hands* and *safe keeping*, it becomes the *dead hand* of the past. In the famous words of G. K. Chesterton and Jaroslav Pelikan, tradition as "the living faith of the dead" becomes "the dead faith of the living."[2] The Iroquois tribe have a maxim, "What would be good for the next seven generations?" Whereas Americans think only of the next business quarter or the next election cycle. Behind traditional attitudes was the simple bet that the combined wisdom of the ages outweighs the best wisdom of any single generation. Every individual human dies, and all human institutions lose energy over time, but living tradition is the deepest human way to defeat death and entropy (outmatched of course by the resurrecting and reviving power of God).

Sixth, generationalism parallels radical modern individualism and reinforces the naivety and utopianism of many modern views of human nature. The idea that each generation starts with a new, fresh, clean slate, colored only by its own experiences is blind to a simple fact. "No man is an island, entire of itself" as John Donne insisted, and neither is any generation. Among other things, sin and its consequences link generations with an unbreakable bond and remind us that we are all pieces of a larger continent and links in a longer chain. Like it or not, choices have consequences and the relationship between the generations is unbreakable at some level. Often for better, sometimes for worse, the old saying was right: the deepest things passed down in families do not appear in the will.

The "sins of the fathers" work their way out in their children and their children's children.

In *The Warriors Honor*, Michael Ignatieff captures the negative side of this truth in his analysis of the ferocity of recent ethnic and sectarian violence. No generation carries a clean slate into its new era. Each inherits its people's past, with all their wounds, insults and humiliations, real or perceived. Thus, whether we are talking of terrorists around the world or certain activist groups in the West, we must face the fact that a major cause of global conflict is the spirit of vengeance carried over from one wound to another and from one generation to the next. Violence is intergenerational. Revenge, Ignatieff concludes, "is a desire to keep faith with the dead, to honor their memory by taking up their cause where they left off. Revenge keeps faith between generations; the violence it engenders is a ritual form of respect for the community's dead—therein lies its legitimacy."[3] At the end of his novel *The Buried Giant*, Kazuo Ishiguro raises a haunting question. There is a certain mercy in the amnesia that covers the wounds of the past like a mist, but what if the mist clears and memory returns? "Who knows what will come when quick-tongued men make ancient grievances rhyme with fresh desire for land and conquest?"[4]

For all these reasons generationalism should be a crucial concern to any group of people that depends on a successful handing on of tradition, whether a family, a business, democratic nations such as Britain and the United States, or the Christian church itself. Needless to say, transmission from generation to generation is at the very heart of the Christian faith, as it was earlier of Judaism, and it is so because of the character of God himself. God reveals himself as the great "I AM," or more accurately as "I WILL BE WHO I WILL BE," and he adds immediately: "This is My name forever . . . to all generations" (Ex 3:14-15). Simply, ultimately and forever, God is "He who is." He is the ultimately free one, who will be what he will be, constrained only by his own character and covenant, but unbound by space and by the passing of time. Creator of all else, including space and time, he is "THE LORD GOD, THE ALMIGHTY, WHO WAS AND WHO IS AND WHO IS TO COME" (Rev 4:8). Jesus our Lord is "the same yesterday and today and forever (Heb 13:8).

This truth throbs at the heart of the Jewish and Christian faiths. When Moses renews God's covenant with the people before he dies, he expressly addresses future generations as well as those standing in front of him: "Now not with you alone am I making this covenant and this oath, but both with those who stand here with us today in the presence of the LORD our God and with *those who are not with us here today*" (Deut 29:14-15, emphasis added to include future generations also present before God). There was no greater captain of history in his time than King Nebuchadnezzar, but even he was forced to admit the fleeting frailty of his mighty empire when compared with the Lord: "His kingdom is an everlasting kingdom / And His dominion is from generation to generation" (Dan 4:3). No wonder the Hebrew psalmist cries out, "Lord, You have been our dwelling place in all generations" (Ps 90:1). This means that our current generational attitudes run directly counter to who we know God to be and directly counter to the biblical view of the generations that in their turn pass before the face of God like armies on parade. But if we have a problem, as we do, the Bible's view of revival also addresses it with hope. Healing is never purely individualistic. It covers the generations too. "He will restore the hearts of the fathers to *their* children and the hearts of the children to their fathers, so that I will not come and smite the land with a curse" (Mal 4:6).

In this grand biblical view, generations are the pulse beats of humanity, and every generation is close to God and responsible to God for its own times, and the transmission from one to another is as crucial to the people of God as it is to humanity at large. Woe betide the family, the nation or the church that fails to pass on its best and its wisest to the next generation! This healthy Christian view of transmission between the generations shines when compared with other religions and most certainly in comparison with secularism. Arthur Koestler's atheism was an extreme case, but his intense promiscuity was allied to his adamant commitment to "no children," as was his later suicide pact with his completely healthy third wife, Cynthia Jefferies. Both were a direct consequence of his atheism and its lack of a wider sympathy for others and solidarity across the generations. (As his English friends described him, Koestler came from "Havington" and not from "Givington.") Today there is a new appreciation of the link between faith and fertility, and it is dramatically clear among the Jews, as the contrast between secular Jews and Orthodox Jews demonstrates. Those who pursue a life with no *Amen* have less invested in the future, and they also have strikingly fewer children. Whereas those who trust in God have the courage to bring new life into the world, regardless of the darkness of the times they live in.

Needless to say, we have a huge disparity toward tradition and transmission within the Christian traditions too—between, say, Orthodoxy and Catholicism on one side and Protestant liberalism and Evangelicalism on the other. Continuity and change are both inherent and unavoidable in history, yet the Orthodox and the Catholics favor the former and Protestant liberals and Evangelicals the latter. The liberals have taken this to suicidal extremes, as I argued earlier, and there is literally no future for the extremes of liberal revisionism. But many Evangelicals are unbalanced too and appear to be foolishly allergic to anything that smells of what they fear is traditional in a negative sense.

Historians say that the sacred music of the Christian church, such as that of Palestrina, Allegri and Tallis, is one of the greatest gifts of the gospel to Western civilization and on par with the splendor of the magnificent European cathedrals, such as Chartres and Lincoln. Yet this rich treasury is an unknown world to many Evangelicals, whose worship music often draws only from songs written after 2000 and does not even include the rich heritage of Celtic Ireland, St. Francis of Assisi, Isaac Watts, Charles Wesley and Fanny Crosby. Thank God for magnificent exceptions, such as the rich, deep hymns of Keith Getty and Stuart Townend, which will join the music of the ages. But much of the run-of-the-mill renewal songs, which are repeated endlessly and constructed more on rhythm than melody, confine Evangelicals within a shallow theology, threadbare worship, fleeting relevance and historical amnesia. Along with soft preaching and a general rage for innovation, such music is another reason why many Evangelical churches resemble a field of quick-growing, quick-disappearing mushrooms rather than a longstanding forest of oaks. Again and again I have been regaled with the church growth maxim, "You have to sacrifice one generation to reach the next." But this turns on a false assumption, and it leads to the telling fact that the fatal weakness of Evangelical church growth is succession. Church growth "success" without succession will always prove a failure in the end.

THERE WILL ALWAYS BE DIFFERENCES

How then do we think through the challenge of healthy tradition in an age that favors incessant change and relentless innovation, and talks of nothing but progress and relevance—and suffers from generationalism? We must begin by openly facing the fact that there will always be tensions and differences between generations. Needless to say, the core reason for Jews and Christians lies in the fall. If sin is the claim to "the right to myself" and to "my view of things," then the tension between the generations simply plays that out on a generational level. The individual's *I* is inflated to the generation's *we*. The prophet's attack on those who say, "I am, who but I?" is transferred to the generation that claims the same. "We are, and who but we?"

But this reminder also leads to what the Spanish philosopher Miguel de Unamuno called the "tragic sense of life." And here, the Jewish and Christian worldviews agree with the classical worldview. Because of the presence of sin, the passing of time and the primacy of the human heart, nothing human is forever. "The grass withers, the flower fades," says Isaiah (Is 40:8). "You cannot step into the same river twice," Heraclitus says. There is always a present generation, a generation coming and another generation going. And each in its turn, without exception, will follow the speeding arrow of time and hear the great auctioneer's cry, "Going, Going, Gone!"

We are aware today of three things that hasten this passing and ensure that any new generation is likely to be restive with the one before. The first is *routinization*, the process through which everything, however revolutionary, fresh, shocking or bizarre, comes to be accepted as routine, taken for granted and therefore ripe to be rejected by the next generation. To be sure, the routine of good habits builds character and virtue (Alexis de Tocqueville's "habits of the heart"). But bad habits build what William Blake called "mind-forged manacles" and at their worst, addictions. I remember a sign in the Australian outback, "Choose your rut carefully. You will be in it for the next 400 miles!" In the same way, success all too easily breeds complacency, a fear of risk and a preference for the comfortable rather than the challenging—and the routines that become ruts.

In the days when the term *man* was still generic and stood for all humanity, it was said that the dynamic of nonprofit organizations went from man to men, to movement and on to monument. A leader with vision, who saw that something fresh was required to meet some need in the world, was followed by others who joined him or her and supported the vision. Together, they created a movement that started with dynamism but faded over time until it ended as a monument—with the fading, sepia-toned photographs of the founders and earlier heroes still hanging in the boardroom. Just so, dynamic organizations wear out their usefulness, and the most creative and radical leaders of fashion become conformist and prisoners of their own once-revolutionary style. A key agenda of most Christian nonprofits should be to succeed and to do so by putting themselves out of a job by feeding their strengths back into the church as a whole.

The second factor that makes the generational tensions endemic is *specialization*, which again is sometimes good and sometimes bad. Generalists were once admired for the extraordinary range of things they knew and could do—for example, the encyclopedic wisdom of Solomon and Aristotle, or the multitalented brilliance of Leonardo da Vinci. But there are few Renaissance thinkers today, and for the last two centuries the specialist has risen to the top of the pecking order. Specialization was reinforced by such ideas as Adam Smith's stress on the division of labor in capitalism, the academic specialization of the German research university and the celebrated ten-thousand-hours principle in the arts. But whatever its genuine benefits, the Achilles' heel of this approach is obvious. Specialization requires a concentration and narrowing, so it will always tend to focus on the greatest strengths, the greatest rewards and the greatest success—and in the process it will prepare the virtuoso for the peaks of his or her chosen goals, but limit them to that and render them next to useless in others. Witness the company boss without his staff, the senior politician without his aides or the president without his teleprompter. In short, specialization too often leads to a loss of the sense of the whole, to a loss of flexibility and to openness toward the spontaneous and the new.

The third factor aggravating the tensions between the generations is *corruption*. "All power tends to corrupt," Lord Acton said famously, "Absolute power corrupts absolutely." But it is not only power that corrupts. Possessions can corrupt too, whether material possessions such as money, property or market share, or immaterial possessions such as status and reputation. With both power and possessions, there is a tendency toward the same progression: moving from accumulation to preservation and then to monopolization, and finally to corruption. The simple litmus test is change and our attitudes to it. When change occurs, those who have the most are those who have the most to lose, and it then becomes obvious whether we have power and we own our possessions, or our possessions have the power and they own us. To those who cling to power and possessions, there is a healthy reminder in Kris Kristofferson's famous line, "Freedom's just another word for nothin' left to lose."[5]

Put these three factors together, and they show why all generations are more flawed than they realize—and naturally, the next generation knows it and wants to go beyond it. No generation is ever as successful and healthy as it may imagine. It always has flaws that set up the next generation to react against the old one, just as the "old one" did to their predecessors when they were the "younger generation." Every generation must therefore be realistic and humble, and the young just as much as the old. Intergenerational tension is inevitable. The old were all once young, and one day all the young will be old. It does not take long before the vanguard becomes the old guard, the self-professed emergents will have long emerged and disappeared in their turn, and the best and brightest of the golden youth will have aged and died. For Christians this appreciation should never lead to weariness or cynicism, but it means that the hope that overcomes it must be solidly anchored in realism. Generations too are touched by life in the fallen world.

WHY NOW?

If the overall reason for the tension between generations is obvious, the obvious question regarding generationalism is, why now? What is behind the generationalism that is prevalent in our time? A leading factor is the accelerated speed of modern life and the accompanying shift in awareness from the importance of the past to the importance of the future. Put simply, as life speeds up, the past seems farther and farther away, including the almost immediate past of our parents and grandparents. In 1969 the anthropologist Margaret Mead gave a lecture in New York that was hailed as revolutionary at the time. The sixties generation was experiencing a historic shift. "There are now no elders who know more than the young themselves about what the young are experiencing."[6] As any grandparents, and now parents, can attest, that insight has become unmistakable in the age of the Internet and smart devices.

In fact, that idea had been around for some time, usually expressed in various ways such as the claim that there has been more change in the last thirty years than in the previous three hundred or three thousand. For example, C. S. Lewis observed that Samuel Johnson in the eighteenth century was closer to Seneca in the first century than to Lewis's generation in the twentieth century. Today, after the coming of the Internet, the same might be said of Lewis as it will be of any of us in a few years time, but it would be pointless to argue about the details of such claims. What matters are the overall consequences. The rapid acceleration of life has led to a serious discounting of the past, including an absurd "anti-oldies" movement.

Sigmund Freud and his notion of the Oedipus complex issued a rallying cry for such attitudes and provided the rationale for all who wish to be impeccably and incessantly progressive. The son must kill the father, and the younger generation must always kill off the older in order to find itself. Contrary to Freud, the problem is not that the father diverts the mother's attention but that the son resents the father's authority. The effect, however, is the same. Anyone stronger than we are is automatically the tyrant, and anyone who is older than we are is automatically the past, so the sure path to the future is to reject them decisively. Incredibly, it was a British Tory cabinet minister—in other words, an ostensible conservative—who trumpeted the cry of the anti-oldies movement: "Someone needs to fight the selfish, shortsighted old. They are the past, not the future."[7]

What this means is that for many modern people "What has the future ever done for us?" is now joined to "What can the past ever say to us?" The result is a stress on change at the expense of continuity, innovation at the expense of tradition, the emergent at the expense of the historic, and the relevant at the expense of the reliable and proven. Needless to say, from the vantage point of the future, all we who are alive today are the past and therefore irrelevant by definition. Yet the truth is that without the wisdom of the past, the young can be as every bit as selfish and shortsighted as the old.

Another factor behind the rise of generationalism is the erosion of older and more solid and objective forms of personal identity. Part of the overall shift from the traditional world to the modern world is the transition from a *thick* sense of community to a *thin* sense of association. Along with it there has been a transition from identity viewed as something ascribed to identity viewed as something achieved. Put simply, as modern people we are no longer defined by our family, our city, our class, our occupation or even our gender. We can be whoever we want to be, and there is an almost limitless range of choices before us—now including more than fifty different sexual orientations to choose from. In sum, modern identity is fluid rather than fixed and invented rather than inherited. The trend is toward the subjective, the shifting and the self-chosen.

Closely allied to this second factor is a third: the impact of consumerism. Behind the rise of modern consumer societies are two basic shifts. One, which took place centuries ago, was the shift from clothes, originally considered garments that were to be functional and lasting, to fashions, which were to be constantly changing as the wearer wished and could afford—originally the preserve of the royals and the nobles, but now of almost everyone. (Sociologist George Simmel described fashion as "the art of becoming.") The other was the twentieth-century shift from production to consumption. Prior to then, production was slow and limited because products were handmade, so consumption was able to keep up easily with production. But with the booming of the Industrial Revolution, production was able to outstrip consumption by far, so marketing and public relations were invented to stimulate consumption.

The result was the mighty engine of the consumer revolution in the last century. Christians rarely put consumerism alongside obviously dangerous ideas such as relativism, but is there any doubt that its damage has been just as severe—and all the more so because it is less noticed? Hilary of Poitiers, the so-called Athanasius of the West, put the point clearly in the fourth century, long before modern consumerism:

> We are fighting today against a wily persecutor, an insinuating enemy . . . who does not scourge the back, but tickles the belly, who does not condemn to life but enriches to death, who instead of thrusting men into the liberty of prison, honors them in the slavery of the palace . . . who does not cut off the head with the sword, but slays the soul with gold.[8]

Among the many consequences of consumerism, two affect the rise of generationalism directly. First, consumer societies represent an insatiable drive for constant change and therefore for a rapid turnover through instant obsolescence. Everything, including the sense of generations, is a matter of fashion and therefore *in* or *out*, *hot* or *cold*, *tomorrow's world today* or *so yesterday*. And second, consumerism becomes a leading way of expressing identity. From the jeans we wear to the car we drive, to the music we listen to, to the credit card we flash in a restaurant, everything says who we are, or we wish to be thought to be. We are what we buy, and like our buying we are changing all the time.

As so often the exception proves the rule and demonstrates it with clarity. The prestigious Swiss watchmaker Patek Philippe advertises its watches with a tasteful picture of a prosperous father and his son, followed by the line, "You never actually own a Patek Philippe. You merely look after it for the next generation." The ad succeeds because it is so strikingly different. With almost everything else, you hardly own it, or own it for very long, because it does not last, or it goes out of fashion and you quickly chase after something newer. Whatever the product, you are the consumer and you are meant to *consume* it, whether food, clothes or cars. It is soon gone, and consumption literally means eaten up, devoured and gone. So too, it appears, with turnover of the generations.

WHAT IT TAKES TO HAND ON THE BATON

How are we as Christians to respond to this lopsided modern trend toward generationalism? First, we must refuse to bow to the idols of change that are at the core of generationalism. Our Lord spoke of "new wineskins" for new wine, so we are wholeheartedly committed to change, to innovation, to enterprise and to risk. But he also warned of what happens when people are stupid enough to use a new patch of cloth to repair an old garment, so we value continuity as well as change and tradition as well as innovation (Mt 9:16-17). In each case, one emphasis without the other is unbalanced and destructive. No one will ever be so innovative that they can stave off decline forever.

One obvious idol of change is the Enlightenment brand of revolution, which was secular and utopian, and openly demonstrated all its flaws in the French, Russian and Chinese revolutions—though not the American Revolution, which in contrast was a conservative revolution. The Enlightenment revolutions overemphasized the capacity of reason, put an unwarranted confidence in the hope of a complete change of human nature and made the political mistake of thinking that they could work from the outside in, rather than inside out, with change that begins with the human heart. Koestler recalled how as an eighteen-year-old he celebrated the triumph of communism in Hungary and passionately sang the "Internationale." ("To wipe out the past forever / O army of slaves, follow us. / We shall lift the globe from its axis, we are nothing, we shall be all.") Later, disillusioned by the dark fruit of such utopianism, he described his trust in Marxist revolution as "the God that failed."

With the passing of the grand age of revolution, today's chief idol of change is the dream of perpetual youth. On one of my first trips to China as an adult, an old gentleman said to me with a wry smile, "You have made a bad mistake. You grew up in China where they only respected age, and now you will grow old in America where they only respect youth. You should have done it the other way around."

His point was sound, though much of the advanced modern world has followed America in its attitudes toward youth, as will China before long. With the greatly extended and privileged time we give to adolescence in the modern world, and with our emphasis on fitness, health and enhancements, and our general denial of aging and death, we tend to forget some simple truths. One is that maturity is relative. It is said that gymnasts are old at twenty, boxers at thirty-five, cricketers and baseball players at forty. Yet doctoral students are old at thirty, while young as professors at thirty-one. Novelists, we are told, do their best work in their twenties and thirties, whereas painters are still young in their forties. Most leaders of the great revivals and awakenings were under the age of thirty, but many of the greatest leaders of nations have been in their eighties. Golda Meir only became prime minister of Israel at the age of eighty. In short, the way of excellence as well as contentment is to be "our utmost for God's highest" at whatever age we are.

Another truth we tend to forget is that many things in life are better with age. Only a fool or an ignoramus would prefer a Beaujolais Nouveau to a vintage Burgundy. In the same way, the foolishness of the 1960s slogan, "Don't trust anyone over thirty," was given its deserved comeuppance in Thomas Oden's brilliant quip, "Don't trust anyone under three hundred." When Andras Schaff, the virtuoso Hungarian pianist, played a sixtieth birthday concert in London, he chose to perform Beethoven's "Diabelli Variations." He had waited until he was fifty, he said, to play Beethoven's thirty-two sonatas. And only after he had performed twenty complete cycles of the sonatas would he dare to move on to the "Diabelli Variations." "It's the most wonderful, the most colorful composition Beethoven ever wrote. . . . I cannot understand pianists who are 20 years old and they immediately play that piece. It cannot be serious."[9] Another pianist, Artur Schnabel, remarked similarly, "Mozart sonatas are 'too easy for children, and too difficult for adults.'"[10]

TRANSMITTING INSTITUTIONS

Second, we must renew our appreciation of what healthy tradition and successful transmission require in social terms. The crux of the matter is that the basic nurturing institutions of any society are also its basic transmitting institutions—the family, the church and the school. It goes without saying that all three are under assault today, and none more than the family. In the Bible's view, the family matters because relationships matter, and relationships matter because God is a person. He is not a philosophical abstraction, an impersonal ground of being, or the sum total of the forces of the universe. So he cares about the personal relationships of those he has made in his own image. Before his chosen people were a people, let alone a nation, they were a family, the family of Abraham and the children of Israel. We therefore honor God above all in our relationships, starting with the family and our neighbors and then moving outward to the wider world.

Needless to say, although the Bible's story starts at the family level, it does not stop there and it does not airbrush the problems of the human family after the fall. It begins with Genesis and the story of a family before it moves to Exodus and the story of a nation, but both of them were repeatedly dysfunctional and anything but airbrushed. All that is before the Old Testament climaxes with Isaiah and the prophets and their vision of the nations and messianic peace. In other words, families prefigure societies and precede states. So the Bible goes from the personal to the public and from the individual to the national and the international. It cares more about quality of the relationships we are in than the kind of regime we are under, for the personal always affects the political more than the political the personal. The character of our society always says more about us than the category of state we belong to. Among other things, this means that families have more to say about freedom, justice and stability than democracy.

This emphasis means that in the biblical view, the family is vital not only as the place where we grow and learn life, but as the bedrock of all our personal relationships and the school where we gain the key to all other relationships—including our political relationships. The love-loyalty of covenant commitment that is fostered by the family will be the measure of the covenant loyalty that we show at the national level, and that covenant love-loyalty will always be a far deeper bond than anything created by Rousseau's social contract or today's narrowly legal contracts.

The opposite is true too. Not even the best of governments can compensate for a broken society with broken families, and a broken society with broken families will produce the government it deserves, which will not be the best of governments. Yet if the Bible focuses on the family, it does not sugarcoat family life. Take, for example, the sibling rivalries of Cain and Abel, Esau and Jacob, and Amnon and Absalom. But the realism of the story is told to advance the interests of the family, and that realism is quite different from the ruthlessness with which advanced modernity has used realism to smash the family to smithereens, along with the covenant love-loyalty of its bonds. The very givenness of the family itself has been destroyed in the name of anything-goes social constructedness, and covenant loyalty has been overwhelmed by non-committal, non-binding choices so that the modern family and the very basis of its cohesion have been devastated.

TWO ESSENTIALS

To be sure, the crisis of generationalism is downstream to the crisis of the family, and it is easy to see why. The plain truth is that we humans live on only through our children and our children's children, so at a minimum there are two essentials if healthy transmission between the generations is to remain healthy and not grow toxic. Both essentials are in diminishing supply today.

First, we need to pass on healthy relationships that are largely free of generational baggage and generational cycles. Today, by contrast, the measure of our broken relationships is one measure of the wideness of the generation gap and the prevalence of the victim culture that thrives on the memory of the sins of the past, whether real or perceived. Witness the preening virtue of today's politically correct puritans who are seeking to avenge all the sins of the fathers from centuries ago. As I write, President Woodrow Wilson and colonial explorer Cecil Rhodes are the two latest "greats" who are currently under the gun and threatened with the downfall of their statuary.

The problem with today's new puritans lies in the fact that the market for flawed heroes is now overheated in terms of both supply and demand. The supply of potential culprits will always be boundless, for we are all sinners, and we have all committed sins that someone somewhere can track down and avenge in the name of justice. What makes this explosive is that in a culture of victimhood, hyper-sensitivity and litigiousness, the demand is equally stoked. But our brave new activists only make the problem worse, for the more the revenge, the greater the resentment, and the greater the need for further revenge. Revenge does not resolve injustice, it recycles it and binds the generations together in iron links of resentment and hatred. What is forgotten is that, even with the direst injustice, judgment alone cannot bring justice and genuine peace unless there is also healing, forgiveness and reconciliation. A society that is bent on avenging all the sins of the fathers (and mothers) will find that they end with no freedom and no future but only the bondage of deepening intergenerational cycles of injury, resentment and vengeance.

Second, it requires two of a certain kind to make the love that makes the children that makes any passing on possible. Do we need reminding that there is not a single human being anywhere or at any time who did not have both a mother and a father? Nor can any marriage without a mother and a father ever become a generator of ongoing life. Natural marriage between a man and a woman is therefore essential for healthy and sustainable societies, whereas genderless marriage is suicidal for a society in the long run. Natural marriage is, after all, the only form of marriage that spans the two basic gaps in human anthropology—the gender gap between male and female and the generation gap between parents and children.

All this means that the crisis of the natural family represents a crisis for freedom, a crisis for the transmission of culture and a crisis for civilization. The French philosopher Hypolite Taine described the family as "the only cure for death," and in the same vein the Swiss theologian Emil Brunner observed that the fifth commandment (on honoring parents) is the Magna Carta of tradition.[11] The overall crisis of the family needs no exposition. From permissiveness of the hookup culture to the pill that separates sexual pleasure and procreation, to no-fault divorce, to abortion on demand, to alternative forms of marriage, to assisted suicide, to the collapse of the family dining table, and to all the sex education materials for students in public schools, all these recent trends have joined forces to undermine the Jewish and Christian view of the family as the bedrock nurturing and transmitting institution of civilization.

If we are to believe the cheerleaders for the sexual revolution and what it is they are out to teach our children, sex is now only for fun with your friends, so experiment freely within the sole proviso of mutual consent. Parents, after all, are no longer the primary educators for their own children. They have no right to interfere with relationships, and marriage and families are irrelevant as anything other than one more lifestyle choice among others. Against such dangerous fantasies, the truth stands that to the degree that these follies continue, our societies will face unprecedented psychological confusion, social chaos and eventual loss of liberty. With the family devastated through the disaster of such deliberate cultural change, cultural transmission and tradition will be the losers too, and with them our civilization itself. But will enough people think twice before it becomes too late?

REMEMBER, REMEMBER

Third, we must remember the spiritual requirements for remaining faithful from generation to generation. Secular tips for staying mentally fresh and innovative are two a penny today, and whole businesses and websites are dedicated to the cause. Curiosity, travel, history, lifelong learning, a resolute commitment to work on problems are some of the most recommended approaches, along with countless commercial offers of medical supplements, memory stimulants and of course today's fashionable essential: brain food.

Our first and last resort, however, must be the biblical approaches to transmission, for the challenge of successful transmission runs like a thread through the Scriptures. It need hardly be stressed that the Bible is a story, the grandest of stories with countless smaller stories within it. Like all stories, it has a beginning and an end and therefore depends on development and on continuity. So it is with faith down the centuries. With its characteristic candor, the Bible openly recounts the dramatic failures in transmission from one generation to the next. Eli's sons were corrupt, Samuel's unfaithful to his example, King David's wayward and rebellious, and Solomon's arrogantly foolish. The Bible gives no sugar coating to its heroes, and there is no airbrushing of the record.

At the same time we are given dramatic accounts of the momentous gravity of transmission, both for individuals and for the nation of Israel. If Israel is to sustain its high calling, faithfulness must be passed on down the generations faithfully. The kings must be faithful to the Lord as the best of their ancestors were. The prophet's mantle must be picked up by another prophet. The torch's flame must be handed over burning brightly. There must be no dropping of the baton. So Moses hands over to Joshua, Joshua to his successors, Samuel to Saul, David to Solomon, Elijah to Elisha and the apostle Paul to Timothy, his son in the faith. Through it all, certain themes ring out again and again, and they are as relevant to us as they were those many centuries ago.

First, those handing over the torch must challenge their successors to *recognize the moment*. Great leaders have an instinctive feeling for the history of their nation and the significance of their moment. It is time to move on, Moses said to Joshua and the people. They had been wandering around in the wilderness too long. It is time to finish the task of occupation, Joshua said to his successors. God has set the whole land before them. The task of the leader's farewell address is not to try and cement their legacy, like the shamelessness of a modern American president's bid for his place in history. It is to set the agenda for the next generation, both in describing the horizon of the moment and drawing attention to its opportunities and challenges for the next generation. That similar task for our own day is urgent.

Second, those handing over the torch must challenge their successors to *remember the road they had traveled*. In the Scriptures, memory has nothing to do with mere mental recall, nostalgia or restored brainpower. It is all to do with gratitude, humility, trust and hope. God has never let us down, and he will never let us down, but we need to remember how he has led us so far. Hudson Taylor, the great missionary pioneer in China, was famous for stressing both *Ebenezer* (to this point God has helped us) and *Jehovah Jireh* (the Lord will see to it and provide in the future). Sin, in contrast, is always linked to forgetting in the Bible. "Remember this day," Moses charges the Israelites, the day after the Passover as they marched out free from Egypt (Ex 13:3). Years later, he adds to the charge as he hands over to Joshua and the next generation. "You shall remember all the way which the LORD your God has led you in the wilderness" (Deut 8:2). "Beware that you do not forget the LORD your God" (Deut 8:11).

So the Jewish celebration of the "Lord's night" begins with the question from the youngest child, which is the annual aid to memory and gratitude, "Why is this night different from all other nights?" So Jacob on his travels raised his pillar to God at Bethel, and so too Joshua and the people left their memorial stones in the Jordan on the day God led them to cross the river and enter the

Promised Land. *Non nobis Domine*—"Not to us, O Lord, not to us, but to your name be the glory!" Whether we are individuals, families, churches or nations, we must keep on telling the story, we must never forget, and we must raise our own family memorials and our national memorials, for memory is the key to gratitude and renewed trust.

Third, those handing over the torch must challenge their successors to *rely on the enduring truths of God's faithfulness*. The best and most successful of humans die. The strongest and most loving families do not last forever. The sunniest and most glorious of times all end in the end. Even the most powerful revivals do not last more than a generation or two. There is no day on which the sun will not set, and no heroism whose luster will not fade. But God's character never changes, God's covenant is unbreakable from his side, God's compassion is unfailing, and God's deliverances, visitations and revivals are always ready. "I am about to die," Joseph said to his brothers, "but God will surely take care of you" (Gen 50:24). We may stake our existence on God against all human opposition and even against the ravages of time and death, "but God." God keeps faith with us even when we lie in the dust, for as the refrain of the psalmist rings out in gratitude, "For his lovingkindness is everlasting" (Ps 136).

The Christian church, and Evangelicals especially, must face up to modern generationalism and break with it. We must discern and demolish its idols and repair its spreading damage. We must restore our own healthy practice of Christian tradition and renew its life-giving transmission that reflects the character of the Lord, whom we worship. We are each significant, but we are only links in the longer chain, notes in the grander melody and pages in the larger story. In the long succession of the generations of faith that stretch back to our Lord himself, there are few more critical links than that of the present generation to the next—because of the particular crisis of our time. What we hand on to coming generations at such a time as this will be especially critical. But as ever, our first priority must be to ensure that what we pass on is fully faithful to our Lord and worthy of being handed over to the next generation—for his sake as well as theirs.

⇒ A Prayer ⇐

O LORD, YOU HAVE been our dwelling place from generation to generation, forgive us when we fall for the selfishness and short-sightedness of our own time. Grant that we may see both our smallness and our significance before you. Grant that we may appreciate our dependence on all who have gone before us, both in our own families and in your church, and at the same time live with responsibility for those who will come after us. Above all, may we so live out our callings before you in our time that, like King David, it may be said of us that we served your purpose in our generation. Through Jesus Christ our Lord, Amen.

QUESTIONS FOR DISCUSSION

1. Do you personally lean toward the innovative or the conservative? How about your family, and your church? What are the advantages and disadvantages of this bias? Where might you need to lead a more balanced life?

2. Draw up a balance sheet of the features of your own generation as you see it. What are its strengths and weaknesses, considered in the light of the priorities of the kingdom?

3. What practical customs or practices might you introduce in your family or your church to ensure a healthy passing on to the next generation of all you have been given and perhaps take for granted?

chapter seven

Give Us the Tools

In April 1963, President Kennedy conferred honorary citizenship of the United States on Winston Churchill and praised him for his immortal speeches—"He mobilized the English language and sent it into battle." Today, decades after World War II, many people can still quote sentences or paragraphs from the prime minister's most famous addresses, such as, "I have nothing to offer but blood, toil, tears and sweat," "This was their finest hour" and "Never in the history of human conflict has so much been owed by so many to so few." Fully deserved though this praise is, it can give a false impression to those who do not have a more fully rounded impression of Churchill. He was eloquent, but he was also far more than just an eloquent orator.

Churchill downplayed his own achievement in speaking. Ten years after the war he said that it was the nation that "had the lion's heart," and he merely "had the luck to be called upon to give the roar." The truth was that all his speeches were the product of immense hard work—first in overcoming his childhood lisp and then in the painstaking crafting of each talk. He wrote every word of every speech, pored over them with care before delivery and would have scorned the speechwriters and teleprompters of presidents today.

At the same time, Churchill's eloquence was simply one part of his exuberant lifestyle, his prodigious capacity for work, his energetic pace of life and his strategic thinking. Not that he had the slightest patience with the modern concern for fitness and exercise. He drank champagne and whisky freely, he smoked cigars, and he once gave the advice to a young man, "Never stand up when you can sit down, and never sit down when you can lie down." Much of his morning work, reading the mail, perusing the newspapers and responding to letters, was done from his bed. Key to his day was his famous hour- or hour-and-half-long siesta at 5 p.m., a habit he had learned in Cuba, after which he was invigorated to work until 2 or 3 a.m. Working like this, he claimed, allowed him to work two solid eight-hour days in every twenty-four hours.

All that and more can be heard in one of Churchill's most famous speeches, delivered in February 1941. In wartime, he said, what mattered was "deeds, not words." He then gave a magisterial tour of the different theaters of war and rose to a crescendo in his appeal to President Franklin Roosevelt and the United States to abandon their policy of isolation and provide the desperately practical help that was needed to combat Hitler. "We shall not fail or falter; we shall not weaken or tire. Neither the sudden shock of battle, nor the long-drawn trials of vigilance and exertion will wear us down. Give us the tools, and we will finish the job."[1]

TECHNOLOGY IS NOT ENOUGH

Deeds, and not words only, are what the church requires today, but what are the tools we need as Christians to engage effectively with the advanced modern world we are facing? There are two essential requirements that go without saying—which of course means that they need to be said, because what goes without saying is too often left unsaid and then forgotten. What we need above all in the church today is for each Christian to have a profound personal knowledge and experience of God himself and a deep knowledge of the Scriptures as his authoritative Word. No one and nothing else can ever replace those essentials. Knowing God himself is the heart of the Christian faith, and knowing God in unmistakable reality. These two things are essentials; though it would be an insult to describe them as tools. But right there we have to acknowledge two immediate problems. One is that the modern church still includes too many nominal Christians, and the other is that we are seeing a growing biblical illiteracy in the church today.

The church will always include nominal, conventional and cultural forms of churchgoers, and their numbers will swell or fall according to the church's standing in society at large. There are times when the consequences of so many nominal Christians are limited, but now is not such a time. So it is not the unrelieved disaster many believe it is when they read the opinion polls and see the rising number of religious "nones." In most cases, it is the old *nominals* who are becoming the new *nones*, a symptom of the diminished standing of the Christian faith in Western culture and the rising power and prestige of secularism. Jesus himself faced a similar situation in his own ministry as he set his face toward Jerusalem and the cross. In earlier and easier times he pointed out that "he who is not against us is for us," but as he came nearer to the cross and the stakes mounted, he reversed the maxim: "he who is not with Me is against Me" (Mk 9:40; Mt 12:30).

In the same way, we are seeing a massive but necessary sifting of nominal Christians today, and the process of clarification is long overdue. It happens at different times in different countries—in the 1960s for the British churches and in the present decade for the United States. When this happens, the middle ground vanishes; it becomes clear that the day of the pew filler and the fence sitter is over; and the stakes are high. In crisis times there is always a cost to discipleship. Have we picked up our crosses to follow Jesus wherever he leads, or are we only along for the ride so long as the fashionable crowds still come to church in droves?

The problem of biblical illiteracy is equally troubling. In his book *What is Judaism?*, Emile Fackenheim, the distinguished Jewish scholar and holocaust survivor, tells of a picture that was hanging in his parents' home in Germany. It was of old, bearded Jews fleeing for their lives from a pogrom and clutching what was most precious to them. "In the view of antisemites these Jews would doubtless be cluching bags of gold. In fact, each of them carries a Torah scroll."[2]

There are similar stories of Christians prizing the Bible in countries such as China where it was banned by the government. There was once a time when the Bible was similarly precious to Evangelicals, when *Bible believing* was almost a synonym for *Evangelical*, when no Evangelical would begin their day without reading and studying the Scriptures, and the best of Evangelical scholars were distinguished for their able exposition and brilliant defense of the Scriptures. Today, however, a rash of factors has changed that beyond recognition—soft preaching, diminished book reading, online information, overbusy lives, the confusion resulting from the superabundance of versions of the Bible, the special pleading of interpretations intended to fit the sexual revolution, and the general shallowness of movement Evangelicalism—and now the truth is that Evangelicals as a whole are no longer distinguished for their deep and faithful knowledge of the Scriptures.

Biblical literacy is not a tool; it is an essential of the faith. But what are the tools and the weapons we need to grapple with the forces we have examined—whether the hostile ideas of the modern world or the shaping power of the advanced modern world itself? The first thing to say is that tools and weapons are much more than technology and techniques, and we need much more than improved technology and techniques to prevail against our challenges. Technology has become one of the leading idols of our age, because its brilliance, its power and the cornucopia of its blessings are as-tonishing—so much so that it takes our breath away, and our com-mitment to it becomes unquestioning and naive. Christians are not Luddites. There is no going back. The Christian faith and its ever-new wineskins have a capacity for progress, reform and change that no other religion or worldview has ever matched. But while we are not curmudgeons, we are not mindless cheerleaders either. All change must be thought through with care and with a strong Christian mind brought to bear on the issues. Early adopters must be discerning adopters.

This is not the place for a Christian critique of the place of tech-nology in the future. Suffice it to say that we must resist all forms of the idolatry of technology and guard against three features in particular. First, technology contains a gnostic tendency that em-phasizes information and the mind and therefore downplays the body. (It is telling that the future promised us by the scientist-kings is always a matter of minds, intelligence and information, and never with anything to do with bodies.) Second, technology has a ten-dency to automate so much of life that it undermines human agency and responsibility. Third, technology, with its seeming neutrality, tends to rule out questions of right and wrong from consideration. But technology's very status as an idol reminds us that modernity magnifies evil, so that even the techno-utopias of tomorrow will suffer from the same crooked timber of humanity that has dogged all human endeavor since the fall.

Perhaps the most pressing naivety to avoid is the way in which Christians place too much reliance on technology in communica-tions. It is true that the communications revolution has opened unprecedented doors of opportunity for the gospel. Never in all human history has communication been more powerful, more ac-cessible and, in the case of media such as the Internet, more af-fordable. We have shifted, it is pointed out, from the communication of "the few to the many" (the grand age of newspapers, radio and television) to "the many to the many" (the new age of the social media). We can therefore expect and welcome a thousand innovative ways of communicating the faith to the modern world.

But we will be frustrated and then disappointed if we do not also recognize the oddities of communicating in the great age of communication. For one thing, the modern world is suffering from inattention. Everybody is now speaking and nobody is listening— or at least listening with focused attention. With more information produced in the last decade than in all previous history, more and more is coming at us faster and faster, and all diced into tiny fragments. For another thing, all words are suffering from inflation. With more and more available, less and less is valuable. Postmodern philosophies have untethered words from any clear content, let alone objective meaning, and they can now be used in any way a speaker likes. At the same time, advertising, commercials and infomercials have reduced words to "words, words, words" and mere empty verbiage. Churchill warned in 1926 that "Words, which are on proper occasions the most powerful engines, lose their weight and power and values when they are not backed by fact or winged by truth, when they are obviously the expression of a strong feeling, and not related in any way to the actual facts of the situation."[3]

For yet another thing, modern communication has its own inbuilt biases toward relativism. Search engines, for instance, customize information, so that even there we have somewhat tailored truth or "news that will best suit you." It purports to be free but is paid for by the advertisers who help shape the presentation too. Last, the Niagara of information and data that cataracts down on us now as facts, metrics, data, big data, opinions and breaking news means that we are devotees of the cult of information and we suffer from information bias. What *soul* was in the Christian era, *information* is today—the inner spirit or essence of everything. It is therefore harder than ever to try to take our information to the level of knowledge, and harder still to take it to the level of wisdom.

The truth is that the power of modern communication has reached an astounding level, and it will only rise higher still. But if we use it without thinking for ourselves, without conscious reliance on the Holy Spirit, without the backing of face-to-face relationships and without love, we will still amount to no more than St. Paul's tinkling cymbals and clanging gongs (1 Cor 13:1). Technology alone will never be enough for Christian communication. All these challenges in communication require much greater consideration, but at least they underscore the danger of the breathless-adopter cheerleader attitude. T. S. Eliot saw the beginning of what we are now facing, and raised the questions,

> Where is the wisdom we have lost in knowledge?
> Where is the knowledge we have lost in information?[4]

Privacy is harder than ever when everyone is invited to be linked in, connected and transparent to others (including hackers and the government), but it matters. Reading books is time consuming, but it matters. Reflection is easily drowned out when life is fired at us point-blank, but it matters. Independent thinking is hard when the social media reinforce groupthink, but it matters. Thinking for ourselves is difficult when it is so much easier to download an expert opinion, but it is essential to the freedom of our own agency, so it matters. Conversations with an iron-sharpens-iron quality are rarer when minds seek carbon-copy approval from others in their own bubble, but they matter. History is more crucial than ever when the relentless modern focus is on the present and the future, but it matters. The courage to hold unfashionable convictions is more difficult when social media mobs give their thumbs-up or thumbs-down like a Roman emperor, but it matters.

And so it goes. Having the right information is vital, but achieving genuine knowledge is better, and mastering both and then attaining true wisdom is better still. We smile wryly when we hear that to a man with a hammer, everything is a nail, but we forget that our computers and our smart devices do the same with us, but on a far bigger scale. Too many of the hi-tech pioneers and the futurist gurus who work with them appear to be driven only by visions of unbounded technology, astonishing financial profits and visions of utopian futures beyond our imagining. It is up to us to counter such visions with a needed balance and to infuse them with strong values and a corrective wisdom. We Christians must always use our new technologies with gratitude and delight, but only as we are thinking constantly of the best and worst that they do for us and to us—while always remembering that we have never seen and heard God more clearly than the amazing time when he became one of us, lived among us and showed us himself as never before—without any metrics to gauge him and without a single smart device in sight.

THE WEAPONS OF SPIRITUAL WARFARE

What, though, of the tools and weapons we need to discern and engage the advanced modern world? As I stressed in *Renaissance*, the companion to this book, Jesus called us as his followers to be *in* the world, but *not of* the world, a demanding stance that combines closeness along with challenge and creates a dynamic cultural tension with the world that gives the church its unique culture-shaping capacity. Achieving this balance and maintaining this tension is difficult, and it requires three things of Christians: first, engagement with the world; second, discernment of the character of the world; and third, the courage to say no to everything in the world that contradicts the truth and calling of our Lord. Here we are primarily looking at the second requirement, discernment, but we must remember the purpose it serves in our overall calling.

Having engaged the world, but before responding to it, we must discern the character of the world, so that we know what to embrace with gratitude and what to resist with courage.

The first tool we need for this discernment and engagement is the weaponry required for spiritual warfare. Human history has always turned on a tension between power and principle, the forces of might pitted against the forces of right. The tension between power and right(s) is obvious in the modern world too, though rights are increasingly called into question today, whereas power is a constant obsession—what it takes to win it, how to defend it against all comers, how we are to sustain it and the best way to use it to our advantage. The postmodern world is especially focused on power at the expense of principle. Nietzsche rejected any notion of absolute or objective truth and replaced it with the will to power. His French disciple Michel Foucault made a career of analyzing everything in terms of power. So there is hardly a discussion now in which the power factor will not be raised. What is the real agenda here? What are the power relationships in the equation? Whose interests are being served? Whose ox is being gored?

The questions are legitimate, if incomplete. Jesus and the New Testament are also concerned with power. So it is all the more remarkable that, except for isolated parts of the church, this modern emphasis on power has not been countered by the biblical understanding of either wrong worldly power or true supernatural power. Indeed, many Christians have it the wrong way around—they major on worldly power and discount supernatural power. Once again, the reason is obvious: the secularization of the church that we examined in chapter two. The unseen, including supernatural power, has become unreal for many Christians in the West. Bishop Lesslie Newbigin pointed out that if anyone reads the New Testament and looks for words on power, authority, rule or dominion, "we find such words on almost every page. The central phrase of the gospel,

the kingdom of God, is obviously about power, authority, rule."[5]
And all the talk of power climaxes at the supreme point of the cross,
where Jesus claims that, when he dies "the ruler of this world will
be cast out" (Jn 12:31).

Who is Jesus referring to as the ruler of this world? He told Pilate
that the kingdom of which he is king is not of this world. If it were,
he could instantly call down legions of angels to be at his disposal.
So by "ruler of this world," he cannot mean Pilate, Herod or the
Emperor Tiberius. They did not need casting out. They could be left
in the hands of "Father Time," and soon they would each be dead
and gone. No, the real adversary behind these human powers was
the evil one. He was the one who was decisively unmasked, disarmed and cast out by the victory of Jesus on the cross (Col 2:15).

The significance of this claim is mind-boggling. We perhaps
need to pray as the psalmist prayed: "Open my eyes, that I may
behold / Wonderful things from Your law" (Ps 119:18). We know
we are all more culturally shortsighted than we realize, so we need
to have our lenses cleaned and our cataracts removed to be able to
take in what Jesus and the apostles said about the cross, and make
it ours with the appropriate humility and reverence. Can Jesus and
the apostles really be saying that, and do they really mean what
they said? Pilate, Herod, Tiberius, Lenin, Stalin, Hitler, Mao, the
president of the United States, the president of the European
Union, the prime minister of Russia and the party secretary of the
People's Republic of China, all these may wield what to most of us
is unimaginable power. But in the light of the victory of Jesus on
the cross, their power is now hollow, and they are no more than
paper tigers in relation to the real power behind the universe. For
Jesus has unmasked and disarmed the power that was once the
heart of the power behind their power, and he is victorious over all
the cosmic forces of darkness too. But that is only the beginning
of the wonder of what is said. Through the power of the cross and

the resurrection, Jesus has proved stronger and triumphed over the evil one and death itself, and he now has all the principalities and powers at his feet. But wonder of all wonders, he invites us to rise and employ that same power, his supernatural power, as we engage the forces of power in our day.

In this sphere, then, the tools we need are the weapons of spiritual warfare. Writing to the Christians in the major city of Ephesus, St. Paul itemizes the different parts that make up the "full armor of God," such as the breastplate of righteousness, the shield of faith, the helmet of salvation and the sword of the Spirit. Writing to the church in Corinth, he claims that while he can talk and operate on a purely natural and secular plane, he engages spiritual warfare in a different way. On the natural plane Paul says he may appear as human as any other human, and weak to boot, but that is not the way he operates in the spiritual realm. "Though we walk in the flesh, we do not war according to the flesh, for the weapons of our warfare are not of the flesh, but divinely powerful for the destruction of fortresses" (2 Cor 10:3-4).

Paul's extraordinary description and his purpose in introducing it must not be left as a pleasant metaphor or an empty picture of unreality. His general point is clear, though what precisely he meant and how exactly he waged that sort of warfare is not spelled out. But the teaching of Jesus is simpler, more incessant and even more amazing. Again and again Jesus is explicit about the supernatural adversary he faced. But all it takes to defeat him, Jesus says equally repeatedly, is prayer—a simple matter of his followers asking the Father to do the things we pray for as we pray in his name, Jesus. Therein lies the authority, and therein lies the power. Jesus even tells us that we have the authority to "bind" and "loose" things on earth that will then be bound and loosed in heaven (Mt 16:18-19). Which is more stunning? That Jesus gave us his followers such power for us to use for the advance of the kingdom, or that with our chronically unmusical condition we are deaf to his words and barely take him seriously?

Walter Wink describes demons as the "drunk uncle of the twentieth century: we keep them out of sight."[6] But it is not only demons that embarrass us as sophisticated modern people. So too, it seems, does spiritual warfare and all the teaching and practices that go with it. But this is to our immense loss and our weakness in society. As Newbigin concludes, "The principalities and powers are realities. We may not be able to visualize them, to locate them, or to say exactly what they are. But we are foolish if we pretend they do not exist."[7] Fearful of appearing credulous before the world, we are foolish if we dismiss the words of our Lord as incredible. Restoring the art of spiritual warfare is a vital key to a faith that can prevail in the advanced modern world of titanic powers. Thanks to science and technology, human power today staggers the imagination and even threatens the planet and our own survival. But there is a power more powerful than the Promethean forces of our day, and the good news of Jesus is that he offers to make it ours if we will only ask.

TRACING THE ANCESTRY OF IDEAS

The second tool we need for discernment is a grasp of the history of ideas. There is no saying when we might encounter a new idea, a fresh opinion or a suddenly fashionable viewpoint that touches on our faith in some way or another. The idea might appear highly attractive or perhaps shocking, and maybe even threatening. But we have to think it through Christianly, and the first step is always to pause and ask the basic questions we should ask of anything we hear or read:

First, what is being said? Unless we ask this question with care, we may be responding to what we *think* a person said, or even worse still, what we *feel* about what we think the person said—a sure recipe for speaking past each other and creating unnecessary misunderstanding.

Second, is it true? In a day when truth is often overridden, this question is often overlooked, but it is crucial. Many an outrageous claim or bad argument has been stopped in its tracks at this stage by questioning whether it is true or not.

And third, what of it? If we understand what a person is saying and believe it is true, the question then arises, What would be the consequences of what the person is saying? Many a claim falls at this point when its practical outcome is understood.

The history of ideas comes in when we have asked these opening questions and are still left wondering about the claims we have heard. The challenge, then, is to examine the sources of an idea to understand by tracing it back to its setting and its history. "Tell me your story," we often say when we are introduced to someone and we wish to get to know the person better. The same is true of ideas. We can get a good idea of people when we know a little of their family, where they were born, where they grew up, where they went to college or university, and some of the life experiences that have made them who they are. We should never judge people by their background, and the same is true of ideas. An idea may come from a dubious or disreputable source and still be true, so to judge an idea by its source is the genetic fallacy. The source of an idea is one thing, and the truth of an idea is another. A person's philosophy is more than their biography, but their biography is a key part of their philosophy.

There is a serious academic discipline that is called the history of ideas, which was developed by Arthur Lovejoy and pioneered at Johns Hopkins University in the early twentieth century. That is not our concern here. The general idea was first made powerful in Nietzsche's writings and his stress on what he called the "genealogy" of ideas and morals. To understand an idea, you have to know its ancestry and its family tree. As with a river, you have to trace it back to the original spring or springs in order to appreciate the sources that set it on its way. We saw examples of this in earlier chapters. Secularism, for example, can be traced from Democritus and Epicurus in Greece to Lucretius in Rome, to Machiavelli in the Renaissance, to Hobbes in the seventeenth century, to Baron d'Holbach and Diderot in the eighteenth century, and so on. Similarly, the notion of the separation of church and state can be traced from Exodus to Samuel, to Jesus, to Pope Gelasius, to Roger Williams, to Madison and Jefferson, and so on.

This approach becomes important for evaluating modern ideas, because the genealogy goes a long way in helping us to understand the significance of an idea and whether it needs to be engaged with greater or lesser seriousness. For example, the Achilles' heel of many of the Evangelicals who called themselves "emergents" was their uncritical acceptance of postmodernism that bordered on naivety. Their strong reaction to modernism was entirely legitimate, but their espousal of postmodernism was naive. Had they done their due diligence in tracing back its sources—to Nietzsche, Heidegger, Foucault, Derrida and the like—they might have looked at it with eyes wide open and not backed into its arms as they reacted against modernism. The fact is that both modernism and postmodernism have their strengths, but Christians do not agree entirely with either. Both are partly right and both are finally wrong, and an understanding of the history of ideas should have given Christians the clues to help them keep their sure footing and avoid toppling into one pitfall or the other.

CULTURAL ANALYSIS

The third tool we need today is cultural analysis, the ability to describe and assess the culture we are living in, and in particular to gauge the impact of culture on our thinking and behavior. Cultural analysis is an essential tool because it helps us discern the character of the world that our Lord has called us to engage. We are called to be in the world but not of the world and neither worldly nor other-worldly. This challenging demand means we need to know the world we are engaging. We have to assess where it is good, true and beautiful, so that we may celebrate it and use it freely and with gratitude. But we also need to know where it is evil, false and ugly, so that we may avoid the damage of its temptations and evils, and then counter or seek to replace them. In short, we will neither understand the world nor be able to resist worldliness if we make the mistake of viewing it only as a matter of ideas. Cultural analysis is therefore the companion tool to the history of ideas, and equally important, though less understood.

What is the difference between the two tools? The general movement of the history of ideas moves in two directions. It starts with a thinker, and then moves backwards to his or her sources and their settings, and then forward again from the thinker to his or her thoughts and writings, and then on to the impact of these ideas on the wider world. Seen this way, the impact of the history of ideas can be described as the process by which ideas wash down in the rain. Nietzsche, for example, has been immensely influential. So much so that the period after his death was called, "the Nietzsche generation." But now, more than a century later, there are many people who have never even heard of Nietzsche, let alone read one of his books, yet the way they talk of his notions such as *relativism* and *power* almost sounds as if they were quoting him. His ideas have washed down in the rain and we are all drenched in their influence.

Cultural analysis works quite differently. In fact it moves in the opposite direction. It does not start with philosophical ideas at all. It starts with whatever *passes* for knowledge in a community, whatever people think is true because it is completely taken for granted, however ridiculous or ill-considered other people may think it to be. It then analyzes the cultural setting in which people

live and traces the impact of that setting on the way people think—
perhaps without any thinker being involved at all.

What on earth am I talking about? The simplest example of
something that is better analyzed by cultural analysis than by the
history of ideas is time. An unmistakable feature of the advanced
modern world that we all recognize is *fast life*, the 24/7 pressure of
living when life is fired at us point-blank today. But what is behind
it? The answer is clearly not philosophy or any set of ideas at all, but
the clock or watch. "All Westerners have watches," an African saying
runs. "Africans have time." Invented in Europe centuries ago, coor-
dinated through the Industrial Revolution and now made instantaneous through atomic time and the age of the Internet, clock time
has put its stamp on us in the form of fast life, and we are all hurried,
hassled and hustled along by its unforgiving pressure.

How do we use cultural analysis properly? We all accept the
central consequence of the history of ideas—that ideas have consequences. But that is only half the story, and the other half is too
often forgotten. Christians, among others, usually see only one side
of the process, but the influence is not a one-way street. "Ideas have
consequences," yes, but contexts have an impact on ideas too. In
other words, the worlds in which we live have a power to shape our
thinking, and the less we are aware of it, the more likely they are to
shape us unawares.

As with the history of ideas, there is an academic discipline de-
voted to this approach—known as the sociology of knowledge—but
our concern is with the general truth that lies behind the discipline,
rather than the academic issues. One thing is crucial, however, and
that is to distinguish this important discipline from the social constructionism that I criticized in an earlier chapter. Social constructionism says that all our beliefs are socially constructed, *and nothing
more*. They are therefore essentially "fictions" that have been made
solid because they have been socially accepted to the point where

they have reached the status of being regarded as self-evident. This idea is not only radical, and put to radical ends, it is self-contradictory. It cannot be applied to itself without undermining itself.

The sociology of knowledge (and cultural analysis) is more humble. It seeks to analyze how our thinking (what is *thought to be* knowledge in any community) has been shaped by our social setting, but it does not pronounce on the truth or falsity of what we believe. Whether something is true or false is not its business. That question is passed on to philosophy, not sociology. Properly understood in his way, the two tools, history of ideas and cultural analysis, are complimentary and not contradictory. We must learn to use them both, for together they throw light usefully on the whole of life and not just on either ideas alone or culture alone.

THE SIGNS OF THE TIMES

Can these three tools, along with our fervent prayer and deep reliance on spiritual discernment, help us engage the world wisely and well today? That is our challenge, and at such a momentous time. If ever there was a moment in which we needed to recognize "such a time as this" to "test the spirits" (seeing the real nature of things) and to "read the signs of the times" (seeing and interpreting events from the perspective of the kingdom of God), it is now. Our task is to take these well-known phrases out of the airy limbo of cliché and bring them down to the realm of practical, daily experience. If we fail to read the signs of the times, or if we do not try, we may be no better than the Pharisees and Sadducees, whom Jesus attacked as hypocrites: "Do you know how to discern the appearance of the sky, but cannot *discern* the signs of the times?" (Mt 16:3).

Reinhold Niebuhr pointed out that weather forecasting was one of the oldest forms of scientific knowledge, and that even though it is enormously advanced in the age of radar and satellites, "it is still a good symbol of the reliability of man's objective knowledge when he analyzes the processes of nature."[8] But there is a difference between areas of knowledge that are relatively objective and other areas where the bias of human sin and subjectivity come in. Jesus told the Jewish leaders to their faces that they were hypocrites. They demanded signs to authenticate the arrival of the kingdom of God when their self-serving "egoistic form of Messianism," which favored only themselves, meant that they would never read the signs rightly even if they were right in front of their eyes. "The lack of discernment would be due, not to a defect of the mind in calculating the course of history, but to a corruption of the heart, which introduced the confusion of selfish pride into the estimate of historical events."[9] In sum, both they and we face a double problem— the ignorance of the mind and the pride of the heart.

Only the Lord knows history objectively and therefore truly. Our eyes are never neutral, our vantage point is never fully objective, our judgments are never completely certain, we are always a part of the world we observe, and our own selves are always at the center of the world we see and the way we think. History is simply too big, our eyes are too shortsighted, and our hearts are too self-interested for it to be any other way. Our best observations are therefore never other than partial and seen "through a glass, darkly" (1 Cor 13:12 KJV), and our best judgments must always themselves be under judgment. I am not a Prophet with an uppercase P, so what I have argued in this book is not prefaced by "Thus says the Lord." I have thought and wrestled over some of these ideas for years, but they are still only my best judgment and are there to be treated as such.

But surely, if we take our Lord and the Scriptures seriously, if we recognize the liability of our own chronic self-pride, if we ask the Lord to examine our hearts and remove the bias, and if we consciously rely on the Holy Spirit to correct us and to guide us, then we may use the tools we have discussed with humility and with profit. And we may use them not as an end to become better pundits but as the means to be wiser and more faithful servants of Jesus in our engagement with the world and the times in which we live.

➣ A Prayer ➢

O Lord our God, your Word is truth, your ways are good, and in knowing you we find our highest wisdom. Teach us to know you more deeply that we may love you more truly, live more faithfully and learn to think your thoughts after you more humbly and gratefully. And, Lord, may it please you to help us, so that in these complicated and tumultuous times we may be able to read the signs of our times that we may walk wisely in your way and bring glory only to you. Through Jesus Christ our Lord, Amen.

QUESTIONS FOR DISCUSSION

1. What practical new things might you do to ensure you are always growing in your knowledge of God and in your understanding of the Bible and faith?

2. Do you have a healthy diet of reading that puts you in working touch with the ideas of our day that are shaping our societies? Where do you need to balance any deficiencies?

3. How would you describe the "signs of the times" that you think are significant for Christians to recognize today? How do you think that recognizing them should make us live differently?

Afterword

A Time to Stand

"The Chinese people have stood up." Mao Zedong's simple but stirring declaration was his salute to the triumph of the Chinese revolution and the inauguration of the People's Republic of China in Beijing on October 1, 1949. I was eight years old and living in the old Ming Dynasty capital, Nanjing, when my father read the news to me and explained what Mao meant. A wave of persecution was already crashing down on Christians and anyone else who differed from the communist victors. At that stage no one could foresee the tens of millions of Mao's fellow Chinese he would slaughter in the name of his horrendous revolutionary fantasies. But China had stood up. The Chinese people had taken their own fate in their own hands. They had taken back their country and put an end to the long nightmare of their humiliation by European, Japanese and American intruders in the land of the Middle Kingdom.

Centuries earlier, Alexander the Great had declared that "the Persians would always be slaves because they did not know how to say the word No"—words which Winston Churchill quoted to buoy the courage of his fellow countrymen as they faced the overwhelming might of Hitler's Luftwaffe, and for many crucial months had to stand alone against the Nazi onslaught. In shining contrast to Alexander's jibe, the Greeks had always refused to prostrate themselves before Darius and Xerxes and all the trappings of their oriental despotism, just as British diplomats and later Europeans refused to kowtow to the Manchu emperors in Peking. When we humans are "on all fours," we are like the other animals. But standing and walking upright, head held high, is essential to human dignity. We are not born that way, of course, so we have to learn to stand upright and work to maintain that stance against all that life throws at us, including the forces of gravity, age and sickness as life goes on.

When the Lord freed the Israelites from slavery under the Pharaohs, he reminded them of the goal he had for them: "I will also walk among you and be your God, and you shall be My people. . . . I broke the bars of your yoke and made you walk erect" (Lev 26:12-13). Free people stand up. They walk upright, and they kowtow to no one and to nothing. Free people have the courage of their own dignity and convictions. Free people know what is wrong and know how to say no to what is wrong. And no one more so than the impossible people whom God has freed to live and stand and walk free before him. Need we talk of Moses before the Pharaoh, of Phinehas at a time of Israelite corruption, of Daniel and his friends before the might of Babylon and Medo-Persia, or St. Peter and St. Stephen, or Athanasius, Peter Damian, Martin Luther, Thomas Cranmer, Dietrich Bonhoeffer, Dietrich von Hildebrand, Oscar Romero, Karol Wojtyla and countless others?

We all know that at times we are knocked down by life, and that one day we will all be leveled by death itself. But God keeps faith with us even when we lie in the dust, and because Jesus rose from death, we too will rise again. Marvelously, the Greek word for resurrection (*anastasis*) literally means "a standing up again." So the impossible people gain their strength from an impossible God who is greater than all, who can be trusted in all situations and who strengthens his people to stand even against death. Despite everyone and despite everything, we are called to stand, and stand we must as God's impossible people. However sweet the seduction, however popular and powerful the tide, however plausible the different gospel, however scornful or brutal the attacks, and however fearful the threats, impossible people stand, faithful only to Jesus, our Lord and our God. So may it be in our time.

This courage to be distinctively Christian and therefore to live differently must be restored to the heart of Christian faith, just as its equivalent has always been the hallmark of the Jews and the secret of their remarkable survival down the centuries and across the continents. At Mount Sinai, the Lord commanded his people that whatever land they were in, "You shall not worship their gods, nor serve them, nor do according to their deeds" (Ex 23:24). Later, their own prophet Ezekiel reminded them sternly that when they desired to be like other nations, they were thinking of something that simply could not be. God would never allow it. "What comes into your mind will not come about, when you say: 'We will be like the nations'" (Ezek 20:32). As the Jewish sages reminded their people, "The whole world was on one side, and they were on the other."[1] Christians stand with Jews in this calling. For Christians to be the same as everyone else is impossible. Impossible people are called to be different, and different they will be or they will not be Christian.

SAMUEL MOMENT, MOSES MOMENT

But this book is more than a bare call to us as Western Christians to brace ourselves. A time to stand is a time to examine ourselves, a time to repent where we are not what we should be, a time to face up to the full scope of our global challenges, a time to pray for revival and restoration, a time to read "the signs of the times" and to "test the spirits," a time to live differently, a time to act and a time to speak out as we engage the world. Among the many points that might be mentioned in closing this argument, two have pushed to the forefront. The church in the West today stands at what might be called both a "Samuel moment" and a "Moses moment."

In *Renaissance* I argued that the church in the West is facing an "Augustinian moment." Just as St. Augustine lived at the end of the long period of Roman dominance in the Western Empire, so we are living at the end of the long centuries of Western dominance in the world. But that parallel gains its strength only in relationship to history. The *Samuel moment* goes deeper in terms of the church's relationship to a culture that is turning away from its previous influence, but the Moses moment is the deepest of all. Loss of dominance is one thing. Loss of influence is another. But neither compares with the Moses moment, for that concerns the nature of the church's relationship to God himself.

Our Samuel moment. By our Samuel moment I am referring to the choice the church faces if it continues to lose its previous influence as the defining faith of the Western world. The word *if* is important because history is never inevitable. The prophet Samuel was Israel's judge more than a thousand years before Jesus and a pivotal figure who was both the last judge and the prophet who anointed Israel's first two kings, Saul and David. Indeed, he demonstrated Israel's separation of "church and state" (or the distinctions between Israel's "three crowns," or three types of national leader: prophet, priest and king), and he initiated the countercultural role of the prophets, who from his time on were the countercultural corrective that addressed the word of the Lord to the kings, the priests and the nation when they deserted the way of God.

Kingship in Israel was not God's intention for his people, merely a concession. The Lord was their king. But the pressure to have a king came about because of the faithlessness of Samuel's sons and the people's desire to have a king "like all the nations" (1 Sam 8:5). At first Samuel was affronted personally, but God reminded him that God was their king and it was he, not Samuel, whom the people were rejecting. But then God gave him a surprising order. "Now then, listen to their voice; however, you shall solemnly warn them and tell them of the procedure of the king who will reign over them" (1 Sam 8:9).

What then unfolds is remarkable. The people of Israel were wrong to choose a king. They would regret it bitterly at times, and Samuel's predictions came all too true in the end. Jewish society was deeper, older and far more enduring than the Jewish state and is still vital today, having survived the long centuries when there was no state. Jewish society was constituted by God at Sinai and it has lasted four thousand years, whereas the monarchical Jewish state was chosen by the people in order to be like the nations around them, and it lasted only a few hundred years. Apart from David and Solomon, the Jewish state was rarely distinguished and was often a leading source of corruption and oppression. But Samuel follows God's instructions and delivers two powerful messages to the people.

First, Samuel delivers a prophetic word: *You have chosen, so you must live true to your choice.* God would respect their choice, wrong though it was, but they were responsible for the choice, and their choice would come with a steep price. So they were free to choose if they so willed, but they should know the consequences and should count the cost. The kings they chose would abuse their power and exploit their sons and daughters, as indeed they did. Second, Samuel demonstrates this prophetic action: *I have chosen, so I must live true to my calling.* The people's choice was wrong, but God forbid that he, Samuel, should join the people or cease to continue doing what he had been called to do as the prophet of the Lord.

The parallels to our own time are profound. The West has almost severed its roots and destroyed the root system. Led by the voices of antifaith and the lure of false visions of freedom, the West is choosing to forget God and go its own way. At point after point the societies and peoples of the West are squandering their Jewish and Christian heritage, flouting their time-tested traditions and values, and carelessly opting for lifestyles, practices and institutions that rival and even surpass those of pagan Rome. Unless these choices are reversed, the eventual outcome of this path will be degeneracy and the end of the West as a civilization. God's moral and spiritual ecology can no more be violated with impunity than his environmental ecology.

Therefore, like Samuel, we must say the following with boldness and with sorrow to our generation: Leaders and peoples of the West, these are your choices, and these will be your consequences. The choice is yours, but so also will be the consequences. At some point the consequences of your settled choices will be your own judgment, and beyond a shadow of a doubt you will know that you have chosen the consequences. Will that day bring evident justice for the millions of your slaughtered unborn? Will it repay measure for measure the shattered lives of children whose families you have destroyed with your foolish alternatives to the natural family? Will your great god mammon collapse and leave his devotees destitute? Will all the magic arts of your best technology fail and land their worshipers back in a state of Hobbesian raw nature? The future is yet unseen, but you are sowing the wind and you will reap the whirlwind.

Whether the bitter harvest you are reaping will take one decade or several to ripen, that day will surely come, and your judgment will be the consequence of your own settled choice. So we solemnly warn you now. Indeed, we plead with you for your own sake and the sake of your children's children, do not go this way. But, and here is the point made clear, if you do go this way, we will not join you. Let the disaster come, but not through us. For our part we are called as followers of Jesus to be a distinctive people, and we are committed to live differently. We will not worship your gods, and we will not live according to your ways. We will endeavor to live according to a higher law within a society that is now choosing a lower law or no law at all. We are citizens of the City of God and no more than resident aliens in the City of Man.

Our Moses moment. That point must then lead to the third and deepest parallel—our Moses moment. Earlier, when discussing God's glory as the antidote to the cultural meltdown, I mentioned Moses' audacious prayer, "Show me Your glory" (Ex 33:18). No one could see God face to face and live, and Moses did not either. But in the supreme crisis of his life as the leader of his people, he knew that he needed to know all of God that a fallen human being could experience and still live. Nothing else would see him through what lay ahead. But Moses' prayer was not simply for himself. He surely prayed on behalf of his people too. For as the Jewish sages point out, the crisis of the golden calf was not simply that the people had created an idol. It was an idol that was to be an oracle and the mouthpiece of God. Terrified by the direct voice of God at Sinai, which they had found unbearable, and fearing they had lost the mediating voice of Moses, they had panicked and attempted to create their own oracle that could lead them forward through the desert. Their golden calf was wrong, very wrong, but the problem that led to it was real. How could the people know the regular, ongoing presence and voice of God in a manner that was bearable and that would continue even when Moses was not with them to be the mediator?

The answer to that question is the heart of the Moses moment. As Moses bargains with God on behalf of the people, Our Lord, the Great "I AM," He who will be who he will be, the one who is "holy, holy, holy," accommodated to his people and gave them the way to know and experience his very presence among them in a manner that they could bear. In Rabbi Sacks's words, "The holy is that segment of time and space that God has reserved for His presence." Indeed, the holy is the time and place in which "God is experienced as absolute presence."[2] The details of the sabbath, the sanctuary, the sacrifices and the system of rules that followed were important but secondary. For Jews, many of those arrangements disappeared forever with the destruction of the second temple, and for Christians, they were swallowed up even earlier through the coming of Jesus and the Spirit of Jesus, whom Jesus gave to his people after he left.

Such provisions were there to guard the inviolable majesty of the holy as the direct experience of God's absolute presence. Holy days and a holy place, and for Christians the Holy Spirit, were given that we might know and experience the absolute presence of God in unmistakable reality without being overcome—so that we in our turn might be the holy people. That same knowledge, experience and purpose of the holy as the *absolute presence of God* is the indispensable nuclear core of Christian faith as it is of Jewish faith, and there is no deeper need in the church today than holiness. Holiness that is born of living before the absolute presence of God, and not humanly devised cultural boundaries and theological checklists, must be the core of the character of God's impossible people. "Show me your glory" must therefore be our urgent prayer just as it was the prayer of Moses. Only those who know God in unmistakable reality can stand the test of the reality of the world of our day.

In sum, our Western nations have both forgotten God and forgotten where they have come from. Now they are attempting to complete the process of severing the roots of Western civilization, destroying its root system, poisoning its soil and ruining its entire spiritual, moral and social ecology. Our Western societies may persist in forgetting God and rejecting his way. But whatever our societies do around us, we are to remain faithful and keep open the place for God in our living. Our privilege is to host the absolute presence of God and to live the way of Jesus so that our difficult and lonely task as his followers is to be faithful and so to be different and to live differently.

God may stretch out his restraining hand and hold us back from the consequences of our settled choices. In his mercy, he may revive his church, and the Christian faith may flourish once again and provide the working faith of the West, or he may not. That is not for us to know. But our faith in God must always be our defining trust and the compass for our way of life. Living before the absolute presence of God, we are called to be faithful, and therefore unmanipulable, unbribable, undeterrable and unclubbable. We serve an impossible God, and we are to be God's impossible people. Let us then determine and resolve to be so faithful in all the challenges and ordeals the onrushing future brings that it may be said of us that we in our turn have served God's purpose in our generation. So help us God.

⇒ A Prayer ⇐

O LORD, WE HUMBLY bow before you. Without your truth, we are confused and our lives lack meaning. Without your grace, we are lost in our sin and cannot find you or save ourselves. Without your mercy, we are overwhelmed by our smallness. Without your providence, we are overcome by a world that refuses to be transformed according to our endeavors and our ideals. You are our Lord and our Rescuer. Grant us your truth to clear our fog, your grace to restore us when we go wrong, your fresh calling to stir new purpose in our hearts, and above all your love and mercy to help us stand with heads held high—that we may be a people worthy of the high calling of making a home for your divine presence in our world and in our time. Through Jesus Christ our Lord, Amen.

QUESTIONS FOR DISCUSSION

1. What single thing do you need to repent of and put right in light of the challenge to the church in our time?

2. What single item for prayer is now on your heart—for yourself, your family, your church or for your nation?

3. What single new action might you take in order to be a part of God's answer to the present challenges?

Notes

INTRODUCTION: FOUND FAITHFUL

[1] Jonathan Sacks, *Future Tense: Jews, Judaism and Israel in the Twenty-first Century* (New York: Schocken, 2009), 51.

[2] Robert Louis Wilken, *The Christians as the Romans Saw Them* (New Haven, CT: Yale University Press, 1983), 23.

[3] Ibid.

CHAPTER ONE: NEW WORLD, OLD CHALLENGE

[1] George Eliot, quoted in Jonathan Sacks, *Future Tense: Jews, Judaism and Israel in the Twenty-first Century* (New York: Schocken, 2009), 13.

[2] Jonathan Sacks, *Covenant and Conversation: A Weekly Reading of the Jewish Bible—Leviticus* (New Haven, CT: Maggid Books, 2015), 368.

[3] Michael Gove, "In Defence of Christianity," *Spectator*, April 4, 2015, www .spectator.co.uk/2015/04/in-defence-of-christianity.

[4] Jonathan Sacks, *Radical Then, Radical Now: On Being Jewish* (London: Bloomsbury, 2003), x, 191.

[5] Ibid., 193.

[6] Lance Morrow, "1968," *Time*, January 11, 1988, 16.

[7] George F. Will, "1968: Memories that Dim and Differ," *Washington Post*, January 14, 1988, A27.

[8] See for example Jeremy Rifkin, *Algeny* (New York: Viking Press, 1983).

[9] Ibid., 64.

[10] Yuval Noah Harari, *Sapiens: A Brief History of Humankind* (London: Penguin Random House, 2011), 14.

[11] Rifkin, *Algeny*, 5-6.

[12] Antonio Regaldo, "Engineering the Perfect Baby," *MIT Technology Review* 118, no. 3 (May-June 2015): 26.

[13] Mary Midgeley, *Science as Salvation: A Modern Myth and Its Meaning* (London: Routledge, 1992), 29.

[14] Ibid., 146-47.

[15]Paul Davies, *Superforce: The Search for a Grand Unified Theory of Nature* (London: Unwin Paperbacks, 1984), 167.

[16]Michael Walzer, *The Paradox Of Liberation: Secular Revolutions And Religious Counterrevolutions* (New Haven, CT: Yale University Press, 2015), 120.

CHAPTER TWO: THE GREATEST CHALLENGE EVER

[1]Richard Lewontin, review of *The Demon Haunted World: Science as a Candle in the Dark,* by Carl Sagan, *New York Review of Books,* January 9, 1997, www.nybooks.com/articles/1997/01/09/billions-and-billions-of -demons.

[2]Jonathan Sacks, *Covenant and Conversation: A Weekly Reading of the Jewish Bible—Leviticus* (New Milford, CT: Maggid Books, 2015), 5.

[3]Friedrich Nietzsche, *Beyond Good and Evil* (South Kingston, RI: Millennium, 2014), 38.

[4]Eusebius, *Life of Constantine* 4.62.1-3.

[5]Augustine, *Reply to Faustus the Manichaean* 17.3.

[6]Sacks, *Covenant and Conversation,* 16.

[7]Peter L. Berger, "For a World with Windows," in *Against the World for the World,* ed. Peter L. Berger and Richard John Neuhaus (New York: Seabury Press, 1976), 10.

[8]Yuval Noah Harari, *Sapiens: A Brief History of Humankind* (London: Penguin Random House, 2011), 27.

[9]Friedrich Nietzsche, *Thus Spoke Zarathustra,* trans. Thomas Common (Blacksburg, VA: Thrifty, 2009), 22.

[10]Origen, *Against Celsus* 7.4.

[11]Augustine, *City of God* 22.8.

[12]Peter L. Berger, Brigitte Berger and Hansfried Kellner, *The Homeless Mind: Modernization and Consciousness* (New York: Random House, 1973), 77.

CHAPTER THREE: THE WAR OF SPIRITS

[1]Jean d'Alembert and Diderot, quoted in Henry Kissinger, *World Order* (New York: Penguin, 2014), 38-39.

[2]Friedrich Nietzsche, *Ecce Homo: How to Become What You Are,* trans. Duncan Large (Oxford: Oxford University Press, 2007), 88-89.

[3]See Thomas A. Farr, *World and Faith and Freedom: Why International*

Religious Liberty Is Vital to American National Security (New York: Oxford University Press, 2008).

[4]Walter Wink, *Unmasking the Powers: The Invisible Powers That Determine Human Experience* (Philadelphia: Fortress Press, 1986), 1.

[5]Ibid., 5.

[6]Ibid., 4.

[7]Derek Prince, *Pulling Down Strongholds* (New Kensington, PA: Whitaker House, 2013), 33.

[8]George Steiner, *The Portage to San Christobal of A. H.* (Chicago: University of Chicago Press, 1981), 164.

[9]Friedrich Nietzsche, *Thus Spoke Zarathustra*, ed. Adrian Del Carro and Robert Pippin (Cambridge: Cambridge University Press, 2006), 214.

[10]Wink, *Unmasking the Powers*, 95.

[11]Ibid., 87.

[12]Erasmus, quoted in Roger Crowley, *Empires of the Sea* (New York: Random House, 2008), 45.

[13]Suleiman, quoted in ibid.

[14]See, for example, chapter 11 in my *Fool's Talk* (Downers Grove, IL: InterVarsity Press, 2015).

CHAPTER FOUR: EXPLORING THE HEART OF DARKNESS

[1]Aurelio Peccei, *The Human Quality* (Oxford: Pergamon Press, 1977), 60-61.

[2]Ibid., 61.

[3]James Bryce, *The American Commonwealth* (New York: MacMillan, 1895), 2:702.

[4]Ibid., 2:793.

[5]Ibid., 2:794.

[6]John Locke, *A Letter Concerning Toleration* (Seattle: Amazon Digital Services, 2012), 50.

[7]Will Durant and Ariel Durant, *The Lessons of History* (New York: MJF Books, 1968), 51.

[8]Karl Marx and Friedrich Engels, *The Communist Manifesto* (Huntington, WV: Empire Books, 2011), 4.

[9]Milan Kundera, *The Unbearable Lightness of Being* (New York: Harper Perennial, 2009), 256.

[10]See, for example, Zygmunt Bauman, *Liquid Modernity* (Cambridge: Polity Press, 2000).

[11]Peccei, *Human Quality*, 15, 17, 22.

[12]Blaise Pascal, *Pensées* 60, trans. A. J. Krailsheimer (New York: Penguin, 1966), 46.

[13]Yuval Noah Harari, *Sapiens: A Brief History of Humankind* (London: Penguin Random House, 2011), 31.

[14]Ibid., 150.

[15]Thomas Hobbes, *Leviathan* 1.6.

[16]Harari, *Sapiens*, 122.

[17]Peccei, *Human Quality*, 129-30, 149.

[18]Ibid., 149.

[19]Christopher Dawson, *Medieval Essays* (Washington, DC: Catholic University of America Press, 1984), 137.

[20]Winston Churchill, "Their Finest Hour," speech to the House of Commons, June 18, 1940, www.historyplace.com/speeches/churchill -hour.htm.

[21]Steven Pinker, quoted in Matthew Beard, "Bioethics Is a Moral Imperative, Mr. Pinker!," *Mercatornet*, August 4, 2015, www.mercatornet.com /articles/view/bioethics-is-a-moral-imperative/16620.

[22]Harari, *Sapiens*, 461.

[23]Paul Ricoeur, quoted in Peter Watson, *The Age of Nothing: How We Have Sought to Live Since the Death of God* (London: Weidenfeld & Nicholson, 2014), 300.

[24]Martin Heidegger, "Only a God Can Save Us," *Der Spiegel*, May 31, 1976, 209, www.ditext.com/heidegger/interview.html.

[25]Harari, *Sapiens*, 415.

[26]Friedrich Nietzsche, *Thus Spake Zarathustra*, quoted in Henri de Lubac, *The Drama of Atheist Humanism* (1949; repr., San Francisco: Ignatius Press, 1995), 501.

[27]Winston Churchill, "Never Despair," speech to the House of Commons, March 1, 1955, www.winstonchurchill.org/resources/speeches/235-1946 -1963-elder-statesman/102-never-despair.

CHAPTER FIVE: LIFE WITH NO AMEN

[1]Jürgen Habermas, quoted in Peter Watson, *The Age of Nothing: How We Have Sought to Live Since the Death of God* (London: Weidenfeld & Nicholson, 2014), 2.

[2]Ibid., 3.

[3]Friedrich Nietzsche, *The Antichrist* 18, trans. R J. Hollingdale; Richard Dawkins, *The God Delusion* (New York: Mariner Books, 2006), 51.

[4]Fyodor Dostoevsky, *The Adolescent*, trans. Richard Pevear and Larissa Volokhonsky (New York: Alfred A. Knopf, 2003), 373

[5]Christopher Dawson, *Beyond Politics* (New York: Sheed & Ward, 1939), 3.

[6]Ibid., 113.

[7]Sam Harris, *The End of Faith: Religion, Terror and the Future of Reason* (New York: Norton, 2005), 52-53.

[8]Ludwig Wittgenstein, *Tractatus Logico-Philosophicus* 6.41 (1922; repr., New York: Cosimo, 2007), 105.

[9]Thomas Nagel, *Mind and Cosmos: Why the Materialist Neo-Darwinian Conception of Nature Is Almost Certainly False* (New York: Oxford University Press, 2012).

[10]Friedrich Nietzsche, *The Gay Science*, trans. Walter Kaufmann (New York: Random House, 1974), 132.

[11]Watson, *Age of Nothing*, 4; Thomas Nagel, *The Last Word* (New York: Oxford University Press, 1977), 130; and Kurt Gödel, cited in David Berlinski, *The Devil's Delusion: Atheism and Its Scientific Pretensions* (New York: Basic Books, 2002), 2.

[12]Watson, Age of Nothing, 5.

[13]Michael Walzer, *The Paradox Of Liberation: Secular Revolutions And Religious Counterrevolutions* (New Haven, CT: Yale University Press, 2015), ix, xii.

[14]Jamie Foxx and Louis Farrakhan, quoted in Benjamin Wiker, *Worshipping the State: How Liberalism Became Our State Religion* (Washington, DC: Regnery, 2013), 1, 5-6.

[15]Henry Lewis, *Modern Rationalism as Seen at Work in Its Biographies* (London: SPCK, 1913), 359.

[16]Watson, *Age of Nothing*, 233.

[17]Peter Shaffer, *Equus*, act 2 (New York: Scribner, 2002), 81.

[18]Iris Murdoch, quoted in Watson, *Age of Nothing*, front matter.

[19]Nietzsche, *The Gay Science*, 108.

[20]Henri De Lubac, *The Drama of Atheist Humanism* (San Francisco: Ignatius Press, 1995), 506.

[21]Quoted in Owen Chadwick, *The Secularization of the European Mind in the Nineteenth Century* (Cambridge: Cambridge University Press, 1975), 214.

[22]Emile Durkheim, *The Elementary Forms of the Religious Life*, trans. J.W. Swain (London: Collier-MacMillan, 1961), 474.

[23]Christopher Lasch, "The Me Decade: Narcissism in America" (Washington, DC: The Hoover Reporting Company, 1979), 32.

[24]Montaigne, quoted Paul Rahe, *Republics Ancient and Modern: Classical Republicanism and the American Revolution* (Chapel Hill: University of North Carolina Press, 1992), 236.

[25]Ovid, quoted in ibid., 283.

[26]Cesare Cremonini, quoted in ibid., 237.

[27]Friedrich Nietzsche, *Will To Power*, trans. Walter Kaufmann and R. J. Hollingdale (New York: Random House, 1968), 145.

[28]Bertrand Russell, quoted in Watson, *Age of Nothing*, 315.

[29]Vladimir Lenin, quoted in ibid., 220.

[30]Emil Brunner, *Christianity and Civilisation* (London: Nisbet, 1949), 105.

[31]Friedrich Nietzsche, *The Gay Science*, 273.

[32]Christopher Dawson, *The Dividing of Christendom* (San Francisco: Ignatius Press, 2008), 31.

[33]See Os Guinness, *The Global Public Square: Religion and the Making of a World Safe for Diversity* (Downers Grove, IL: InterVarsity Press, 2013).

[34]See Brian Tierny, *The Crisis of Church and State* (Englewood Cliffs, NJ: Prentice-Hall, 1980), 13; and John M. Barry, *Roger Williams and the Creation of the American Soul* (New York: Viking Penguin, 2012).

[35]Guinness, *Global Public Square*, 200-203.

CHAPTER SIX: YESTERDAY, TODAY, FOREVER

[1]Henri De Lubac, *The Drama Of Atheist Humanism* (San Francisco: Ignatius Press, 1995), 331.

[2]See G. K. Chesterton, "The Ethics of Elfland," chap. 4 in *Orthodoxy*; Jaroslav Pelikan, *The Vindication of Tradition* (New Haven, CT: Yale University Press, 1984), 65.

[3]Michael Ignatieff, *The Warrior's Honour* (New York: Henry Holt, 1997), 188.

[4]Kazuo Ishiguro, *The Buried Giant* (New York: Alfred A. Knopf, 2015), 297.

[5]Kris Kristofferson and Fred Foster, "Me and Bobby McGee," BNA 69035, 1969.

[6]Margaret Mead, *Culture and Commitment* (New York: Doubleday, 1970), 64.

[7]Chris Huhne, quoted in Des Wilson, "Why I Fear Our Next War Will Be Against Our Own Children," *Daily Mail*, May 18, 2014, www.dailymail

.co.uk/news/article-2631251/Why-I-fear-war-against-children-A-drain
-society-Clogging-homes-Soaking-state-cash-routine-insults-hurled
-pensioners-resentful-young-Now-one-senior-writer-enough.html.

[8]Hilary of Poitiers, quoted Christopher Dawson, *The Making of Europe: An Introduction to the History of European Unity* (Washington, DC: Catholic University of America Press, 1954), 48.

[9]Andras Schaff, quoted in Tim Franks, "Andras Schaff: Why I Won't Perform in Hungary," *BBC World Service*, December 22, 2013, www.bbc.com/news /magazine-25450716.

[10]Artur Schnabel, quoted in ibid.

[11]Erik Kuehnelt-Leddihin, *Liberty or Equality* (Auburn, AL: Mises Institute, 2012), 275; Emil Brunner, *Christianity and Civilisation* (London: Nisbet, 1949).

CHAPTER SEVEN: GIVE US THE TOOLS

[1]Winston Churchill, "Give Us the Tools and We Will Finish the Job," *BBC Radio*, February 9, 1941, www.awesomestories.com/asset/view/Churchill -Give-Us-the-Tools-and-We-Will-Finish-the-Job.

[2]Emil Fackenheim, *What Is Judaism?* (New York: Macmillan, 1987), 60.

[3]Winston Churchill, "Artful Dodger!," in *Never Give In! Winston Churchill's Speeches*, ed. Winston S. Churchill (London: Bloomsbury, 2013), 73. This speech was given in the House of Commons, April 22, 1926.

[4]T. S. Eliot, "Choruses from The Rock," 1934.

[5]Lesslie Newbigin, *Lesslie Newbigin: Missionary Theologian: A Reader*, comp. Paul Weston (London: SPCK, 2006), 39.

[6]Walter Wink, *Unmasking the Powers: The Invisible Powers that Determine Human Experience* (Philadelphia: Fortress Press, 1986), 41.

[7]Newbigin, *Lesslie Newbigin*, 47.

[8]Reinhold Niebuhr, *Discerning the Signs of the Times: Sermons for Today and Tomorrow* (New York: Charles Scribner's, 1946), 2.

[9]Ibid., 4.

AFTERWORD: A TIME TO STAND

[1]Jonathan Sacks, *Radical Then, Radical Now: On Being Jewish* (London: Bloomsbury, 2003), 50.

[2]Jonathan Sacks, *Covenant and Conversation: A Weekly Reading of the Jewish Bible—Leviticus* (New Haven, CT: Maggid Books, 2015), 145.

Name Index

Acton, Lord, 141, 179
Alexander the Great, 157, 215-16
Athanasius, 29, 216
Augustine, 71, 83, 95-96, 218
Ayer, A. J., 86, 144
Basil, 32
Bauman, Zygmunt, 123, 138
Ben-Gurion, David, 79
Berger, Peter, 78, 87, 92
Bismarck, Otto von, 100, 104
Blake, William, 177
Bonhoeffer, Dietrich, 29, 216
Brunner, Emil, 15, 157, 189
Bryce, James, 118-21
Buber, Martin, 96-97
Buckley, William F., 44
Calvin, John, 85
Canning, George, 72, 100
Chesterton, G. K., 14, 78, 172
Churchill, Winston, 15, 136, 139, 195-96, 200, 215
Comte, Auguste, 151
Cremonini, Cesare, 155
d'Alembert, Jean, 90
Damian, Peter, 31-32, 216
Daniel (the prophet), 29, 82, 97-98, 216
Darwin, Charles, 128
Davies, Paul, 50
Dawkins, Richard, 86, 117, 145, 148, 154
Dawson, Christopher, 136,

146-47, 160
Descartes, 154
Diderot, Denis, 90, 154-55, 208
Diogenes the Cynic, 157
Disraeli, Benjamin, 41
Donne, John, 172
Dostoevsky, Fyodor, 12, 146, 172
Dubos, René, 58
Durkheim, Emile, 153
Dworkin, Ronald, 150-51
Einstein, Albert, 92
Eliot, George, 41
Eliot, T. S., 201
Epicurus, 146, 154, 208
Fackenheim, Emile, 198
Farrakhan, Louis, 152
Foucault, Michel, 203, 208
Francis of Assisi, 59, 159, 176
Freud, Sigmund, 156, 180
Frisch, Max, 142
Gelasius, Pope, 163, 208
Gödel, Kurt, 149
Habermas, Jürgen, 142-44, 148, 150, 166
Harari, Yuval, 19, 47, 78, 129, 132
Hardy, Thomas, 52
Harris, Sam, 117, 149, 151
Hegel, George, 10, 122
Heidegger, Martin, 16, 138, 208
Heraclitus, 177
Hitchens, Christopher, 117, 145, 154, 159
Hitler, Adolf, 14, 29, 49,

96, 196, 204, 216
Hobbes, Thomas, 58, 102, 130, 163, 208
Hume, David, 86, 154, 158
Ignatieff, Michael, 173
Ishiguro, Kazuo, 173
Jefferson, Thomas, 110, 132, 162-63, 208
Julian the Apostate, 26, 38
Kant, Immanuel, 90-92, 102, 112-13, 170
Kierkegaard, Søren, 72, 112
Koestler, Arthur, 175, 184
Kristofferson, Kris, 179
Lasch, Christopher, 153
Lenin, Vladimir, 157, 204
Lewis, C. S., 16, 83, 108, 150, 180
Lewontin, Richard, 64
Locke, John, 121
Lot, 74-75
Lukacs, John, 149
Luther, Martin, 29, 216
Machiavelli, 43, 152, 154, 163, 166, 208
Madison, James, 105, 208
Maistre, Joseph de, 120-21
Mao Zedong, 28, 64, 204, 215
Marx, Karl, 11, 121-23, 132, 156
Mead, Margaret, 180
Midgeley, Mary, 50
Mirandola, Pico della, 10, 128
Montaigne, 154
Moses, 34, 75, 93, 107, 112, 127, 174, 190-91, 216, 218,

221-22

Mott, John R., 75
Mumford, Lewis, 47
Murdoch, Iris, 153
Nagel, Thomas, 149-50
Nebuchadnezzar, 29, 93, 174
Newbigin, Lesslie, 203, 206
Niebuhr, Reinhold, 15, 211
Nietzsche, Friedrich, 11, 48, 68, 81, 91-94. 96, 103, 112-13, 117, 122-23, 126, 135, 139, 145-46, 149, 153-54, 156-58, 203, 207-9
Obama, Barack, 92, 121, 152
Oden, Thomas, 185
O'Hair, Madalyn Murray, 104, 144
Origen, 83, 146
Ovid, 154
Packer, J. I., 111
Pascal, 128
Paul (the apostle), 73, 79, 81, 84, 97, 108, 112, 190,

201, 205
Peccei, Aurelio, 17, 116, 135
Pelikan, Jaroslav, 172
Peter (the apostle), 25, 43, 74, 216
Pinker, Steven, 137
Plato, 47, 78, 92
Pliny the Younger, 30
Polkinghorne, John, 148
Prince, Derek, 95
Renan, Ernest, 153
Rifkin, Jeremy, 47
Rilke, Rainer Maria, 152-53
Rousseau, 130-31, 186
Russel, Bertrand, 117, 144, 156-58
Sacks, Jonathan, 20, 41-42, 66, 78, 222
Samuel (the prophet), 162, 190, 208, 218-20
Sartre, Jean-Paul, 157
Schaeffer, Francis, 108
Schaff, Andras, 185
Schnabel, Artur, 185
Shaffer, Peter, 153

Sidgwick, Henry, 152
Simmel, George, 182
Smith, Adam, 58, 98, 178
Spinoza, Benedict, 156
Steiner, George, 96
Stott, John, 34
Taine, Hypolite, 189
Taylor, Hudson, 191
Tocqueville, Alexis de, 118, 177
Unamuno, Miguel de, 177
Valery, Paul, 138
Vidal, Gore, 44
Voltaire, 152, 155
Walzer, Michael, 150
Watson, Peter, 150
Weber, Max, 92
Wesley, John, 58
Williams, Bernard, 149
Wink, Walter, 94, 97, 99, 206
Wittgenstein, Ludwig, 149
Woolf, Virginia, 58
Yeats, W. B., 119

Subject Index

atheism, 83-84, 89, 128, 136, 142-63, 166-68, 175
  new atheists, 41, 64, 102
Catholicism, 31-32, 39, 42, 44, 84, 99, 104, 111-12, 158-60, 175
change, 67, 123-24, 130, 175-76, 181-82, 184
  Christian response to, 70, 87, 179, 183, 199
  cultural, 105, 189
  political, 152, 170
  rapidity of, 125, 171, 180
  social, 170
Christian revisionism, 30, 72, 110-12, 175
communism, 46, 149, 153, 155, 184, 215
consumerism, 68-71, 182-83
death of God, 96, 122-23
differentiation, 76
Enlightenment, 56, 72, 86, 90, 162, 170, 184
Evangelicals, 31-32, 42, 70, 72-74, 106, 111-12, 175-76, 192, 198, 208
evolution, 133, 136
family, 131, 150, 185-87, 189
generationalism, 170-73, 176, 180-83, 187, 192
globalization, 51-52, 54-57, 123
gnosticism, 59, 199
humanism, 27, 135
  evolutionary atheistic humanism, 23,

127-28, 132, 137-39
  liberal humanism, 137
  modern humanism, 139
  new humanism, 135
  socialist humanism, 137
illiberal liberalism, 105, 145
impossible people, 31-32, 96, 216-17, 222-23
industrialization. See revolution
Islam, 23-24, 29, 38, 63, 75, 92, 99, 101-2, 112, 145, 157
Jacobins, 72, 155
Judaism, 25, 34, 42-43, 66, 70, 75, 93, 109, 128, 156, 159, 173, 175, 191, 198, 217, 219, 222
  Jewish and Christian faiths, 22-24, 37-41, 43, 45, 66-67, 93-94, 105, 117, 120, 134, 136-37, 145, 160-62, 174, 176-77, 189, 220, 222
liberalism. See illiberal liberalism
Marxism, 38, 50, 99, 119, 157, 184
modernism, 62, 86-87, 208
modernity, 21-25, 29-30, 40, 55-57, 62-67, 75, 77, 86-88, 101, 122-25, 159, 187, 199
  multiple, 55, 60

  singular, 55
Muslims. See Islam
National Socialism, 21, 30, 99, 119
nihilism, 23
  postliberal secular, 145
nominal Christians, 22, 197
pluralism, 40, 45, 163
  pluralization, 67, 76, 160
postmodernism, 62, 87, 106, 111, 125, 200, 203, 208
postmodernity, 62-63
Protestant liberalism, 72, 110, 175
public square, 103, 145, 161-62, 165-66
realism, 79, 165, 187
Reformation, 85, 159
relativism, 40, 125, 130, 171, 182, 200, 209
Renaissance (book), 33, 202, 218
Renaissance (time period), 128, 154, 178, 208
revisionism. See Christian revisionism
revolution, 119, 184
  American Revolution, 155, 184
  Chinese Revolution, 184, 215
  French Revolution, 41, 106, 151, 155-56, 170, 184
  human revolution, 135
  Industrial Revolution,

46-47, 52, 121-22, 182,
    210
  sexual revolution, 21,
    30, 44, 130-31, 134,
    145, 189, 198
salvation
  in Christianity, 35, 66,
    82, 108, 205, 224
  in humanism, 135, 138
science, 50, 78, 86, 128,
  132, 135-37, 149
secularism, 23-24, 38-40,
  45, 64, 94, 105, 149-51,

160, 165, 175, 197, 208
  progressive
    secularism, 22-23,
    26, 38, 43, 146
  secularization, 24,
    56-57, 64-65, 87, 105,
    118, 150, 203
separationism, 24, 64, 105,
  145, 162-63, 165, 208, 218
singularity, 26, 138
skepticism, 63, 132
social constructionism,
  128-30, 133-34, 210

statism, 24
tradition, 76, 106, 118-20,
  122-24, 143, 150, 176, 181,
  185, 189, 220
  assault on, 130
  Christian, 43, 74, 170,
    175, 192
  generationalism and,
    172-73, 183
  marginalization of, 54
  secular dependence
    on, 164

Scripture Index

OLD TESTAMENT

Genesis
11, *49*
11:6, *49*
19:9, *74*
50:24, *192*

Exodus
3:14-15, *173*
5:2, *107*
10:26, *75*
13:3, *191*
23:24, *217*
33:18, *127, 221*

Leviticus
26:12-13, *216*

Deuteronomy
8:2, *191*
8:11, *191*
29:14-15, *174*

Judges
21:25, *107*

1 Samuel
4:21, *126*
8:5, *219*

8:9, *219*

2 Kings
6:16-17, *79*

Psalms
11:3, *116*
90:1, *174*
119:18, *204*
136, *192*

Isaiah
26:18, *126*
40:8, *177*
57:13, *126*

Jeremiah
12:5, *27*

Ezekiel
20:32, *217*

Daniel
4:3, *174*
4:26, *93*
5:27, *126*

Habakkuk
2:14, *127*

Malachi
4:6, *174*

NEW TESTAMENT

Matthew
9:16-17, *183*
10:7-8, *80*
10:28, *74*
12:30, *197*
16:3, *211*
16:18-19, *205*
26:39, *109*

Mark
9:40, *197*

Luke
3:16, *80*
4:4, *109*
4:18-21, *80*
6:46, *75*
11, *170*
11:29, *170*
11:30, *170*
11:31, *170*
11:32, *170*
11:50, *170*
11:51, *170*
17:33, *74*

John
3:16, *59*
12:31, *204*
12:50, *109*
14:6, *110*
19:10, *95*
19:11, *95*
20:28, *66*

1 Corinthians
2:4, *81*
13:1, *201*
13:12, *212*

2 Corinthians
10:3-4, *205*

Colossians
1:15-16, *79*
2:15, *204*

Hebrews
13:8, *174*

Revelation
4:8, *174*
15:4, *96*
18:19, *96*

Also by Os Guinness

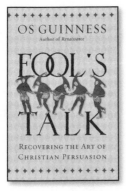

Fool's Talk
978-0-8308-3699-4

A Free People's Suicide
978-0-8308-3465-5

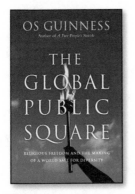

The Global Public Square
978-0-8308-3767-0

Renaissance
978-0-8308-3671-0